The Decentralized Web

AF725924

The Decentralized Web

Building the Next Internet

Navin Sarkhel

Mindful Pages

Published in 2026

ISBN: 9789374597200 (PB)
ISBN: 9789374596579 (eBook)

Published by

Mindful Pages
Imprint of Alpha Editions LLC
312 W. 2nd St #1834
Casper, WY 82601, USA

All rights reserved.
No part of this publication may be reproduced, distributed, or transmitted in any form or by any means — including photocopying, recording, or other electronic or mechanical methods — without the prior written permission of the publisher, except in the case of brief quotations used in reviews or permitted by applicable copyright law.
This book was developed using advanced writing tools to support the drafting and ideation process. All content has been thoughtfully curated, refined, and reviewed to ensure quality and relevance.

Content

Introduction

We live inside a paradox. The web promised boundless connection: friendships that span continents, markets without borders, information at the speed of light. And yet, our digital lives are increasingly confined to a handful of corporate estates. You may spend years building memories on a social platform, documenting your passions, your milestones, your identity—only to discover that, if you leave, you must abandon most of it at the gate. You can export your data, yes, but you cannot meaningfully take it with you. Like a tenant who leaves a furnished flat with no rights to the furniture, your digital possessions remain hostage to the platform that issued them. We have confused participation with ownership, connection with captivity.

Consider the quiet absurdity of the everyday internet. You can send an email to anyone, regardless of which provider they use. Yet if you wish to speak to someone on a modern messaging app, you must first check whether they inhabit the same walled garden. The constraints are artificial, not technical, designed to maximise corporate retention rather than human agency. The web today speaks the language of openness while operating like a collection of exclusive clubs. The irony is painful: never has the world been so networked, yet never has the value of our networks been more enclosed.

This book is born from a simple but radical idea: the internet does not have to be a series of platforms that capture us, but a set of protocols that empower us. Protocols are the hidden agreements that make the web work: HTTP for loading pages, TCP/IP for routing packets, DNS for finding where things live. When these protocols thrive, new innovation flourishes effortlessly on top of them. When platforms dominate, innovation must ask for permission—and users pay the price. In a protocol-led world, your identity, your data, and your creativity travel with you. In a platform-led world, they are privileges granted, not rights possessed.

History shows that the most durable advances in connectivity have seldom come from monopolies wielding power, but from standards shared freely. The email network grew not because a single company orchestrated it, but because anyone could build upon it. The early web was exhilarating precisely because it did not require allegiance to a gatekeeper. We forget that this openness was not guaranteed; it was won through design choices that valued interoperability over extraction. Those choices have been eroded, replaced by convenience that conceals dependency.

There is a deeper story here: the struggle over who shapes our digital future. On one side stand the custodians of Web2, with their meticulously optimised data engines and irresistible user experiences. On the other side is a diverse and sometimes chaotic movement striving to rewrite the rules: decentralised identity, peer-to-peer storage, verifiable computation, user-owned networks. This movement is not a monolith. It contains the earnest and the opportunistic, the visionary and the reckless. Its technologies, often grouped under the term Web3, have been celebrated as revolutionary and dismissed as pointless—sometimes within the same breath. But beneath the noise lies a sincere question that the web must confront: who truly owns the digital world?

Ownership is not merely about property; it is about power. To own your digital identity is to choose where you participate without reintroducing yourself each time like a stranger. To own your data is to carry your digital life with you, enriching whichever services you deem worthy—not the other way around. To own the networks you inhabit is to have a say in their evolution, not merely to click 'Accept' on decisions made elsewhere. These are not utopian abstractions. They are pragmatic questions that determine whether the web will remain a public square or continue to calcify into a series of gated resorts.

Yet decentralisation is not a cure-all. If it were, we would not need a book. Distributing power introduces new fragilities: markets that reward speculation over service, systems vulnerable to coordination failures, responsibilities that once belonged to companies now falling on individuals who are ill-prepared for them. Losing a password can become losing a life's worth of assets. Networks designed to eliminate middlemen may unintentionally recreate them in subtler forms. Trust, long outsourced to institutions, must be rebuilt from protocols and incentives. As we unravel what centralised systems have solved for us, we must understand what they protected us from.

The shift from platforms to protocols is therefore not merely technical; it is cultural. It demands that we rethink what we consider convenient and what we consider fair. It challenges engineers to account for human behaviour, not just cryptographic proofs. It asks policymakers to see beyond the familiar shapes of incumbency. And it invites users—ordinary citizens of the internet—to reclaim agency they may not realise they have lost. This is not about rejecting the infrastructure that sustains today's web, nor pretending that decentralisation automatically yields virtue. It is about designing systems that give people meaningful choice.

Every transformative technology in history begins by reshuffling relationships of power. The printing press unsettled the custodians of knowledge. The telegraph disrupted gatekeepers of communication. The open web upended publishers and retail empires alike. Each shift was accompanied by both optimism and anxiety; neither emotion was misplaced. We now stand on the brink of another such shift, but unlike earlier ones, this time the stakes include the very substrate of our social and economic lives. The internet has become our memory, our marketplace, our public discourse. Whoever governs the architecture of that space governs much more than technology.

This book is a guide for those who want to build systems that respect human dignity and resilience. It does not promise cheerleading or inevitability. It promises clarity. You will learn how decentralised systems achieve trust without gatekeepers—and why that trust can crumble. You will examine tokens as economic coordination tools—when they work and when they devolve into financial theatre. You will explore governance models that distribute decision-making—without assuming that distribution always equals democracy. You will discover how identity, privacy, and data storage can be decentralised—only if we acknowledge the complexity of human lives. Each chapter asks harder questions than the last, because the decisions that shape the future should never be easy.

We will confront the uncomfortable truth that decentralisation is not an absolute virtue, but a spectrum of choices. Some information deserves global consensus; some belongs in the messy privacy of our devices. Some networks should rely on economic incentives; others thrive on social trust. The art is in choosing wisely—and accepting trade-offs openly. Systems fail when promises ignore constraints. Systems endure when design honours reality.

Throughout this journey, a recurring motif will guide us: the distinction between owning and merely accessing. When you own your identity, you carry your reputation across contexts like a trusted passport. When you own your data, you are not forced to rebuild your history on every new platform like a migrant with no paperwork. When you own your place in a network, governance becomes a shared responsibility rather than a distant decree. Ownership, in the digital age, is not possession of a file—it is the ability to assert rights across the entire web.

The choice before us is stark. If we continue along today's trajectory, the internet risks becoming a series of private fiefdoms masquerading as public spaces. If we embrace protocols that return power to the edges, we may yet preserve the internet as a commons: messy, diverse, and resilient. Which outcome prevails depends on decisions made in code, in standards bodies, in companies, and in communities around the world—all in the coming years.

None of this will be achieved by technology alone. Cryptography cannot conjure compassion. Smart contracts cannot resolve human conflict. Automated governance cannot replace attentiveness. The decentralised web must integrate not only new architectures of trust, but new norms of care. It must design for how people actually behave, not how we wish they would. It must accommodate disagreement, error, and evolution. The internet is not merely a machine; it is a society.

So let us ask the questions that matter. What does fairness mean when executed by code? Who protects us when no one owns the system? How do communities govern infrastructure that outlives its founders? Why should a user trust a network they cannot see? And what happens when our desire for autonomy collides with our need for safety?

These are not questions with single answers. They are tensions to navigate, principles to negotiate, values to surface. This book offers you the tools to understand those tensions: the concepts behind consensus and incentives; the economics of tokens; the politics of governance; the human factors of privacy; the pragmatics of interoperability; the craftsmanship of open-source systems; and the experience design that turns possibility into adoption.

The decentralised web is neither a foregone salvation nor a passing fad. It is a proposal. A proposition that we can reshape the internet into something more durable, equitable, and humane. A belief that power should not accumulate invisibly, and that freedom online should be more than the illusion of choice within a set of branded boxes.

We are at a crossroads. To one side lies a future where a few corporations and states decide how billions may interact. To the other lies a distributed, evolving network of protocols that anyone can join, improve, fork, or abandon. Both futures are technically possible. Only one ensures that the web remains ours.

This book is an invitation to look beneath the dashboards and the slogans, to study the scaffolding beneath our digital world, and to participate in its reconstruction. It is a call to curiosity, not certainty. The next internet will not be built by cheering from the sidelines. It will be shaped by the choices of those who understand what is at stake—and who have the courage to demand better.

Let us begin.

Chapter 1
From Platforms to Protocols

Every morning, billions of people wake up and tap the icons that guide their digital routines. A blue bird, a green speech bubble, a familiar red-and-white play button. We rarely pause to question the invisible architecture beneath these symbols. We simply accept that if a friend sends a message from one service, it may reach us only if we inhabit the same service. We accept that if a company shutters a product, the relationships, creations, and communities built within it can vanish overnight. We accept that we live online by permission. The design of the internet has quietly shifted from a public commons into a patchwork of privately-owned kingdoms, and most users barely noticed the gates rising around them.

It was not meant to be like this. The original web was constructed on a radical premise: that any node could speak to any other, that open protocols would act as shared grammar, and that innovation would flourish without requiring approval from a single sovereign. Instead, the current digital landscape is dominated by platforms that aggregate, monetise, and ultimately control the interactions they host. We have convenience beyond imagining, yet our freedom within this immense connectivity has been traded away—sometimes knowingly, often not.

It is tempting to imagine that the history of the web is a tidy progression: decentralised beginnings, inevitable consolidation, and finally, the promise of a return to decentralisation through new technologies. But the truth is messier. Each stage reflects a deliberate set of choices—and compromises—about identity, ownership, and coordination. To understand where we might go, we must first understand how we arrived here.

The Web2 stack emerged to solve genuine problems. Managing identity across sites was a burden; storing and syncing data across devices was hard; payment rails were arcane and fragmented. Platforms stepped in with irresistible offers: log in once, host everything here, click to purchase. They gave us instant access, effortless onboarding, and beautifully polished features. Aggregation was rewarded because unified databases made personalisation and discovery easy. Network effects soon did the rest: the more users joined, the more valuable the platforms became, and the harder it was for anyone to leave.

Imagine you have spent years curating a social profile—a gallery of your relationships and history. The platform allows you to download the raw data, applauding itself for honouring your "portability". But what can you do with it? You cannot import it seamlessly anywhere else. The terms of service protect the platform, not you. Your data is technically yours, but functionally theirs. Contrast this with email: you switch providers without losing your address, your messages continue to flow, and no corporation governs whom you can contact. The underlying protocol—not a platform—defines the network's power.

Protocols, at their core, are agreements. They coordinate behaviour across countless independent actors without needing a central commander. They succeed not through dominance but through interoperability. Consider TCP/IP: no single company owns it, yet it underpins everything. Or think of RSS—once a quiet revolution enabling blogs and news sites to speak a common language. Anyone could subscribe to any source, no gatekeepers required. RSS did not die; it was suppressed by platforms that preferred captive attention to open dissemination. Its rise and fall remind us: the choice of protocol shapes who holds power.

In today's resurgence of decentralised technologies, the word "protocol" has re-entered public discourse, too often accompanied by grand promises and vague explanations. The hype is loud; the architecture is quiet. Yet architecture is what matters. To grasp the significance of this shift, we must read code, not slogans. We must understand what a wallet actually manages, how a node participates in consensus, how a token moves across a network—and what happens when something breaks.

Picture a simple token transfer. A user signs a transaction with their private key, broadcasting it to a network of nodes. These nodes validate the transaction against agreed rules, adding it to the ledger if consensus is reached. The receiving wallet reflects the change. At each step, a protocol defines who can do what: how identity is proven, how validity is judged, how disputes are resolved. This is programmable coordination—trust encoded into rules rather than enforced by intermediaries. But the power of such systems depends on the clarity and discipline of their design. Misplace a rule, and incentives misalign. Misjudge an assumption, and an entire network fractures.

Decentralisation is often misunderstood as a binary: either you are centralised or you are not. Reality defies such simplicity. Communication always faces latency; storage always faces cost; humans always face trade-offs. Global consensus is expensive and slow by necessity; local caching exists precisely because universal agreement about every detail would break the world. Some decisions belong with everyone; others should remain close to those affected. When we speak of decentralisation, we are not flipping a switch—we are tuning a system across multiple axes.

The forces that drove centralisation did not disappear. People want convenience. Businesses want profit. Governments want oversight. Attackers want vulnerabilities. Any attempt to redesign the web must acknowledge these constraints honestly rather than pretend that pure ideology can overcome physics or human nature. Decentralised networks will thrive only when they outperform alternatives where it matters: portability, resilience, fairness, user agency. Otherwise, they risk becoming complex replicas of the systems they sought to replace.

Understanding this distinction—between the platform-led past and the protocol-led future—matters profoundly right now. Our current web is efficient at scale, yet brittle under stress. It enables creativity, yet channels power upwards. It fosters connection, yet isolates communities outside corporate boundaries. If a platform alters its algorithm, entire livelihoods evaporate. If it changes the rules, billions must adjust without recourse. We have built digital dependence on entities that owe us nothing.

The next phase of the internet invites us to rethink that relationship. What if identity were truly portable, a constant companion rather than a new account for every application? What if value transfer required no monopolistic gatekeepers? What if communities could design their own rules, enforceable without central approval? What if services could compete not by hoarding data but by delivering better experiences to free users?

These are not speculative fantasies. They are practical questions emerging from real infrastructures being deployed today. But to build wisely, we must separate durable principles from passing trends. Systems must be designed for how the world is, not how whitepapers wish it would be.

This chapter will dismantle the assumptions that have shaped the web we inherited, exposing both the brilliance of Web2's engineering and the costs embedded within its success. It will show how protocols coordinate us more effectively when they empower choice rather than restrict it. It will cultivate a critical eye, capable of distinguishing architectural substance from branding gloss. And it will illuminate the constants—human behaviour, economic incentives, physical limits—that no amount of technological novelty can erase.

What happens when control shifts from platforms that own our relationships to protocols that merely mediate them? What becomes of innovation when permission is no longer required? How do we prevent new protocols from becoming new platforms in disguise? These questions will define the decades ahead.

Turn the page, and we will look beneath the glossy surfaces of our current digital life, tracing how we moved from the open commons of the early internet to the concentration of power we now inhabit. We will examine how coordination works without a gatekeeper—and why the wrong design choices can sabotage even the noblest intentions. Most importantly, we will begin to understand what it would take to build systems that are not only technically decentralised but meaningfully empowering.

The road from platforms to protocols is not a return to the past. It is a chance to rediscover the web's promise—this time with the lessons of history firmly in mind.

The Stack We Inherited

In September 2006, Facebook opened registration to anyone over the age of thirteen with an email address. Overnight, universities saw a shift from scattered personal blogs and independent message boards to a single social platform headquartered in Menlo Park, California. Friends who had built their identities on their own domains quietly abandoned them. The gravity of a central platform proved too strong. By the end of 2008, Facebook had surpassed 150 million users worldwide (Facebook, 2009). A decade later, this choice would feel irreversible. The web had consolidated. The user had been absorbed.

The promise was irresistible: one login for everything. A button that remembered who you were. Photos accessible from any device. Payments made in seconds. Each of these conveniences solved a genuine frustration from the early web. Managing multiple passwords felt exhausting. Syncing files across devices broke regularly. Buying goods online required trust in merchants scattered across the globe. Platforms stepped in and smoothed the rough edges. The cost of that smoothness, however, was not immediately visible. When identity, data, and payments move into the same vault, whoever owns that vault owns the relationship.

By 2010, a handful of companies governed the majority of digital identity. Google's OAuth system allowed users to "Sign in with Google", turning a corporation into a global passport office. Apple's App Store rules in Cupertino decided which apps could handle payments. Amazon Web Services became the hosting environment for vast numbers of young businesses, based not in a public commons but on private soil. These were not public utilities; they were commercial models executed at planetary scale. Choice remained, technically. But behaviour adhered to gravity. Simpler won.

Aggregation flourished because it delivered benefits that decentralised alternatives could not yet match. Speed. Search. Spam protection. Developers found enormous value in centralised APIs, which offered rich data streams and billions of reachable users. The implicit deal was clear: build here, and we will give you reach—so long as you abide by our terms. The terms could change at any moment.

Consider a case that played out in April 2012, when Twitter altered its API conditions. Third-party clients like Tweetbot and Echofon discovered that features once available were suddenly restricted; user experience was forced to align with Twitter's own app. Developers were warned not to "replicate core Twitter experience" (Twitter, 2012). Innovation that competed with the platform's business interests became a breach rather than a contribution. The protocol had become a platform, and the platform demanded control.

Now contrast that with email. If Google locks your Gmail account, you can migrate to Fastmail or Proton Mail and continue sending and receiving messages to any address in the world. The network's value is not contained inside a corporation but emerges from the *protocol*: SMTP, IMAP, POP. These protocols do not ask for permission. They define interoperability as a right. Email is imperfect—spam, phishing, awkward threading—but it demonstrates what happens when standards, not firms, govern the network.

Email shows us what freedom looks like. Twitter's API shows us what captivity feels like.

Identity followed a similar arc. In the early 2000s, users created discrete identities for each website they joined. It was fragmented, but it kept control local. With the rise of "Sign in with Facebook", the blue button streamlined onboarding and exported social graphs everywhere—until Facebook changed the rules. In 2014, the company limited third-party access to friend data after the Cambridge Analytica revelations. Developers saw their apps break overnight. Users could not authorise the sharing of relationships they believed they owned. Identity was not property; identity was a licence.

Data centralisation became the next inevitability. Cloud storage giants offered redundancy and speed unmatched by peer-to-peer systems, which struggled with reliability. Google Photos launched in May 2015 with "unlimited" free storage, a proposition no distributed network could afford to match. Millions entrusted their most intimate records to a single company, trusting contractual assurances that could be rewritten unilaterally. As the British author E.M. Forster once warned, "Only connect"—but connection without autonomy becomes dependence.

Payments completed the triad of centralisation. PayPal resolved disputes and handled fraud, embedding institution-like trust into a private system. Apple Pay made mobile transactions seamless in London shops by September 2015 after cooperation with major banks. Amazon stored card details that followed shoppers from books to groceries. Each removed friction. Each increased lock-in.

Network effects sealed the arrangement. When all your friends, files, and finances reside within a handful of platforms, leaving becomes a social and economic cost rather than a technical option. The moat is built not of code but of community. Markets that reward centralisation inevitably breed monopolies—not always through predatory power, but through the mathematics of connection.

There were counter-movements. In 2010, Diaspora launched from New York as a decentralised social network backed by grassroots funding. Users could host their own data. No single company stood in charge. And yet the project struggled, not due to ideology but because building a polished, reliable experience without centralisation proved intensely difficult. People chose convenience over autonomy. The tension between freedom and friction has never been resolved.

This is the quiet motif beneath our digital lives: Agility belongs to platforms. Agency belongs to protocols. We have spent the last fifteen years surrendering the latter for the former.

The dependency on platforms shapes behaviour. Influencers adjust content for opaque algorithms. Publishers sculpt headlines for the whims of search engines. App developers abide by 30% fees to access iPhone users. Each choice consolidates power upstream. The invisible hand has been replaced by invisible terms of service.

The Web2 stack excelled at masking complexity. A login button concealed federated authentication systems capable of tracking activity across multiple domains. Cloud dashboards hid global data centres spanning Dublin, Tokyo, and Oregon. Payment gateways wrapped compliance, risk scoring, and chargeback protocols inside a single API call. Efficiency replaced literacy. Users lost sight of how digital society worked—and who directed its norms.

There is a risk in romanticising decentralised beginnings. The early internet was chaotic. Broken links, amateur design, rampant abuse. Platforms solved problems users could not fix alone. They built trust layers the open web lacked. Any honest examination of the future must acknowledge this: centralisation succeeded because it delivered.

Yet success brought new fragilities. When Facebook's DNS configuration error caused a global outage in October 2021, billions lost talk, work, and commerce simultaneously. A single provider represented a single point of failure for human connection. Decentralisation would not have prevented the bug—but it would have prevented the cascade.

Consider the political dimension. When platforms become the public square, corporate policies become speech governance. Decisions about what constitutes misinformation or harmful content are made in boardrooms and implemented by moderators under intense pressure. Rights once upheld by public law drift into private jurisdiction.

Economic incentives intensify these dynamics. Every additional datapoint strengthens a platform's profiling models, driving higher advertising revenue. Every extra account increases switching costs. Doubling down on centralisation is profitable. Building escape hatches for users is not.

Meanwhile, innovation suffers. To create a competing social product, one must rebuild identity networks, data histories, and distribution channels from zero. The incumbent's moat is not excellence alone—it is inertia embodied in billions of choices made in the past.

The discontent now visible across the industry—regulators probing market dominance, consumers questioning data extraction, creators demanding fairer treatment—is a signal. The stack we inherited has reached a point where its benefits are eroded by its constraints. The questions before us no longer concern convenience alone; they concern legitimacy.

What alternative exists? We treat protocols not as legacy infrastructure, but as living machines of coordination. Protocols act like public roads: anyone can travel them, businesses can build around them, and communities can enforce rules through collective agreement. The rise of cryptocurrency and decentralised identity systems represents an attempt—imperfect, uneven—to rebuild autonomy at the architectural level.

But the shift cannot simply reverse the past. New primitives must exceed old platforms where it matters. Reliability must meet or surpass cloud performance. Recovery experiences must surpass forgotten-password flows. Economic models must compete with profitable advertising systems. If autonomy demands sacrifice, most will decline.

The challenge is therefore twofold. First, to identify what must be decentralised: identity, data portability, permission to participate. Second, to accept what centralisation solves well: fraud defence, instant access, seamless interfaces. Users should not feel like network administrators to claim ownership of their digital lives.

As we examine our current position, the erased alternatives deserve acknowledgment. It did not have to be inevitable that one login system would become dominant. It did not have to be inevitable that content distribution would rely on a single feed. Protocols could have been allowed to evolve in parallel with platforms. But investment flowed where returns concentrated: inside fences, not across commons.

Today's centralised systems provide extraordinary value. They also constrain our future. The stack we inherited shows us what happens when convenience accumulates into control. If we want networks that remain open, resilient, and fair, we must revisit the power of agreement—the protocol—not just the allure of aggregation.

A simple question now hangs in the air: when you press a button online—whether to share a thought, store a memory, or send value—who ultimately decides what happens next? The answer determines who truly owns the web.

Protocols as Coordination

At 12:01 a.m. on 1 January 1983, engineers at ARPANET carried out a coordinated transition that would later be known as the "flag day". Machines across the network—stretching from research hubs in California to university laboratories in New York—shut down one protocol stack and activated another. The shift to TCP/IP, designed by Vint Cerf and Bob Kahn at Stanford in 1974, allowed independently operated machines to exchange packets using a shared method of addressing and routing. No single organisation controlled the network's shape or purpose. Yet alignment emerged. The new protocol did not demand obedience; it invited participation. That night demonstrated something profound: coordination at scale need not flow from hierarchy. It can arise through agreement.

Protocols sit in this unusual position between the social and the technical. They are rules, but only insofar as people commit to them. They encode instructions, but only insofar as machines interpret them. They are powerless in isolation and powerful in use. A protocol succeeds when countless actors—engineers, administrators, companies, citizens—accept its grammar and speak it consistently. A protocol fails when that shared commitment fractures. The motif that threads through this history is simple: a handshake. Not the handshake of cryptography alone, but the handshake of cooperation. Each connection is an act of trust extended and reciprocated.

TCP/IP scaled because the handshake held. It offered no proprietary advantage, no exclusive licence. It worked because it created common ground. Organisations in London, Boston, and Tokyo could interconnect without negotiating bespoke integration contracts. The protocol asked only that each participant follow the same rules when sending and receiving packets. The IETF's open Request for Comments process, formalised in the late 1980s, reinforced this ethos. Anyone could propose improvements; decisions were made by "rough consensus and running code". The network rewarded interoperability rather than dominance. That single design choice shaped the internet's trajectory more than any corporate strategy ever could.

The implications of that choice appear in behaviour rather than rhetoric. When a network operator configures a new router, they adopt TCP/IP because it guarantees communication with every other node. When a browser loads a page, it performs the same handshake millions of machines perform daily. These are decisions made silently at the edges, not enforced at the centre. The result is a network that grows through accretion: each new participant strengthens the whole by following the shared ritual.

Other protocols have followed similar paths, though not always with the same endurance. RSS emerged in 1999 when Netscape engineers in Mountain View defined a simple XML-based format for syndicating articles. It allowed any publisher, whether a major newspaper or a single individual writing from a bedroom in Manchester, to distribute updates that any reader could aggregate. Tools like NetNewsWire, released in 2002 in California, exemplified what RSS made possible: a personalised, chronological stream of writing across the open web. The power of this protocol did not lie in any single platform; it lay in the freedom of readers and writers to connect without approval.

RSS reached its cultural peak in the mid-2000s, fuelling the blogosphere and enabling early podcast distribution. Yet its decline reveals the vulnerabilities that open standards face. As large platforms consolidated user attention, they offered features that RSS could not easily match: personalised feeds, integrated comment systems, frictionless re-sharing. When Google shut down Google Reader in July 2013, after operating it from Mountain View for eight years, millions of users lost the central hub through which they had consumed feeds. RSS did not disappear, but its influence waned. It exposed a limitation: protocols flourish when supported by strong incentives, and they falter when those incentives weaken. The handshake must remain valuable.

This contrast between TCP/IP's resilience and RSS's retreat shows the core mechanism behind protocol power. Adoption depends on more than technical design. It depends on the social, economic, and cultural conditions surrounding that design. TCP/IP coordinated the internet because communication requires universality. RSS coordinated publishing only as long as both readers and writers valued independence more than convenience. When behavioural metrics shifted—hours spent inside platforms, not across sites—the gravitational pull of centralisation intensified. The shared handshake loosened.

For every successful protocol, there is a counter-example that reveals the boundaries of coordination. XMPP, an open messaging protocol launched in 1999 by Jeremie Miller in Iowa, allowed federated chat services to interconnect. For a time, Google Talk (released 2005) embraced it, enabling users across domains to exchange messages. It promised a future in which messaging resembled email: portable, interoperable, resilient. But by 2013, Google turned off federation, and the broader industry had pivoted to closed systems. XMPP struggled to deliver features like seamless media sharing and end-to-end encryption at the pace required for mass adoption. The limitation is not a failure of ideals; it is evidence that technical elegance alone cannot outweigh concentrated investment or consumer expectations. The handshake must be both principled and practical.

These examples reveal a deeper truth about coordination: protocols distribute authority by design. When a protocol defines how information flows, it shapes who can build, who can participate, and who can profit. This is not theoretical. It becomes visible in concrete behaviours. A developer builds a new email client without seeking permission because SMTP allows it. A publisher syndicates content through RSS without paying a fee. A researcher inspects a blockchain transaction because the protocol guarantees transparency. Protocols make these rights structural rather than optional.

Once we see protocols as instruments of coordination rather than mere technical artefacts, their influence becomes clearer. They define the boundaries within which innovation occurs. They determine whether power accumulates at the centre or disperses outward. They decide whether modification is an act of contribution or rebellion.

Yet no protocol is neutral. Choices embedded at the outset—addressing formats, governance structures, extension mechanisms—predetermine what is easy and what is difficult. TCP/IP makes spoofing possible without additional safeguards; IPv6 addresses that risk, but adoption has been slow since its publication in 1998. RSS prioritised simplicity, not authentication. XMPP prioritised federation, not rapid feature iteration. These design choices express values as much as technical preferences. They declare which behaviours the network encourages.

The handshake motif resurfaces here: a protocol offers a greeting that others may accept. But not all greetings are equal. Some create stable bonds. Some create fragile alliances. The stability of a protocol depends on how well the incentives of its participants align with the protocol's expectations. Where misalignment appears, fractures follow.

Consider again the ARPANET flag day of 1983. Its success required coordinated action across multiple sites: universities, research labs, military bases. The protocol shift succeeded because participants shared a goal—reliable, scalable communication—and because TCP/IP made that goal feasible. It was an alignment of interest, not an assertion of authority. If any major site had refused the transition, fragmentation would have followed. Instead, the handshake unified.

Compare that with Google Reader's closure in 2013. Nothing in the RSS specification changed. The protocol remained open. But Google's withdrawal removed a crucial point of user engagement. The social incentive diminished. The handshake remained valid, but fewer people extended their hand.

Protocols also embody trade-offs that only become visible when systems scale. TCP/IP's openness allowed unprecedented growth, but it created challenges for attribution, accountability, and security. RSS empowered publishers, but it provided little insight into reader behaviour, reducing its commercial appeal. These effects are not incidental. They arise from design decisions, which in turn express assumptions about the world.

When engineers choose a protocol, whether consciously or incidentally, they choose a distribution of power. This choice shapes future behaviour. Developers adapt to what the protocol rewards. Organisations adapt to what it permits. Users adapt to what it makes simple. Architecture becomes culture.

Protocol choice matters because it establishes the constraints within which institutions and communities operate. A protocol that permits federation encourages diversity of hosts. A protocol that grants unilateral control to a platform encourages concentration. A protocol that treats data as portable encourages competition. A protocol that binds data to a single service encourages lock-in. These are not accidental outcomes; they are manifestations of the protocol's implicit contract.

In decentralised networks, this dynamic intensifies. A protocol that defines how nodes reach consensus determines who can validate transactions and who can build services. A protocol that sets fee structures influences which participants join or leave. The rules of coordination become the rules of power.

The choices ahead, therefore, are not merely technical. They determine whether we build systems that behave like public infrastructure or systems that behave like private estates. They determine whether new protocols inherit the strengths of TCP/IP or the fragilities of RSS. They determine whether the handshake remains mutual or becomes symbolic.

A final question lingers. When we design the next generation of protocols—identity systems, storage schemes, consensus mechanisms—whose incentives will they align with? Will the handshake invite equitable coordination, or will it mask a new centralisation behind the language of openness? The answer depends on the agreements we commit to, and the agreements we refuse.

Hype vs Architecture

On 19 June 2017, the price of a single ether briefly spiked to $319 on the GDAX exchange in San Francisco before collapsing to $0.10 within seconds. A large market sell order triggered a cascade of automated trades. Headlines described the crash as proof of a system unfit for purpose. Yet the incident had little to do with Ethereum's architecture and everything to do with the interface layer: a centralised exchange matching trades off-chain, governed by its own risk controls. The contrast was stark. Public narratives framed a protocol failure. The protocol had not even been involved. It showed how easily the story of a system can overshadow its structure.

Headline-driven narratives flatten technical complexity into slogans. "Decentralised", "trustless", "scalable", "next-generation"—words that acquire an aura detached from the engineering beneath them. Architecture, by contrast, is unembellished. It sits in whitepapers, code repositories, and the behaviour of running nodes. When a developer submits a pull request to a client implementation, they shape the network more than any marketing slogan ever will. Hype is noisy. Architecture is quiet. It endures.

The motif that threads through this section is a window. A window lets you see what is actually happening, not what someone claims is happening. Reading the code is looking through the window. Reading the headlines is staring at a painted façade.

The gap between story and structure becomes most visible when systems fail. In March 2020, as markets convulsed during the first wave of the COVID-19 pandemic, the MakerDAO protocol—launched in December 2017 to maintain a dollar-pegged stablecoin—faced extreme stress. A surge in Ethereum gas prices prevented many bids in its liquidation auctions from executing. Some assets were sold for zero DAI. At a glance, commentators blamed "DeFi risk". But the architectural cause was precise: auction keepers could not submit bids in time because gas prices exceeded their configured thresholds. It was a mismatch between incentive design and network conditions. A technical decision, not a philosophical flaw. The implication was immediate. Protocol resilience requires attention to configuration logic, not headline sentiment.

Architecture diagrams serve as maps through this terrain. They reveal where responsibility lies. Consider the simplest diagram of a token transfer on a proof-of-stake chain like Ethereum (post-Merge, September 2022). At the left edge sits the user's wallet—MetaMask, Rabby, or a hardware device such as a Ledger Nano X. The wallet constructs and signs a transaction using the user's private key. Signing is not magic; it is elliptic curve cryptography implementing the secp256k1 curve. The signed message is broadcast to a local or remote node, often through an RPC endpoint hosted by Infura or Alchemy, both headquartered in the United States and operational since the mid-2010s. That node propagates the transaction across the peer-to-peer gossip network, where validators include it in the next block if it meets fee and validity conditions. Finally, the receiving address reflects the balance change once the block achieves confirmation.

That journey—from wallet to node to validator to state transition—constitutes the architecture. Everything else is commentary.

A slogan like "self-custody is freedom" obscures the subtlety that most wallet users depend heavily on centralised RPC providers. If Infura experiences downtime—as happened briefly in November 2020—millions of wallets cannot broadcast transactions even though the underlying protocol remains fully operational. The slogan claims autonomy. The architecture reveals dependency. The implication is clear. Systems must be evaluated as composites, not symbols.

Ethereum is not unique. Bitcoin, launched in January 2009, has attracted a mythology so strong that it often eclipses its mechanics. Beneath the slogans lies a simple architecture: a UTXO model, SHA-256 hashing, and Nakamoto consensus. The behaviour to observe is a miner committing computational work to produce a valid block header. The decision to accept that header reflects a set of software rules enforced by nodes, not market narratives. When the Bitcoin Cash hard fork occurred in August 2017, the divergence happened because different groups adopted different rule sets. The market followed the architecture. The architecture did not follow the market.

For a counter-example, consider IOTA, launched in 2015 and headquartered initially in Berlin. It introduced the "Tangle", a graph-based ledger that claimed to eliminate miners, reduce fees to zero, and scale without bottlenecks. The rhetoric was ambitious. But architecture introduced a Coordinator node controlled by the foundation to protect the network from attacks. When that node was halted in February 2020 after a security breach in the Trinity wallet, the network effectively froze. The limitation was not theoretical; it was operational. The hype promised decentralisation. The architecture required central oversight. Reconciling this tension demands honesty. Ambition cannot rewrite cryptographic constraints.

The value of studying architecture becomes most evident when mapping how data and authority move through a system. Let us trace, in concrete steps, a basic token transfer—say, sending 1 DAI from a user in London to a friend in Nairobi. The user opens a wallet and selects "Send". The wallet constructs a transaction specifying the DAI contract address, encoded in ABI format, calling the "transfer" function with a destination address and amount. This is visible behaviour: a user clicking a button. The wallet signs the transaction using the private key stored locally or on a hardware device. This is a decision: commit to the action irreversibly. The transaction enters the mempool of a connected node. Miners or validators choose transactions from that pool based on gas price or fee priority. That choice reflects economic incentives, not abstract ideals. A block is produced and propagated. The protocol updates the state, reducing the sender's balance in the DAI contract and increasing the recipient's. The journey completes.

Nothing in that sequence relies on slogans. Everything rests on architecture and incentives.

Whitepapers, too, are windows—though some are smudged. A well-structured whitepaper names its assumptions explicitly: expected network conditions, adversarial models, throughput ceilings. The Bitcoin whitepaper (Nakamoto, 2008) presents a clear threat scenario: an attacker controlling more than 50% of the hashing power could rewrite history. It does not embellish. It measures. By contrast, numerous token sales in 2017 described throughput claims—"millions of transactions per second"—without specifying hardware requirements, network topology, or consistency guarantees. When examined, these claims dissolved. They were façades, not windows.

Architecture forces specificity. It narrows the gap between ambition and reality. It demands that designers quantify latency, bandwidth, and fault tolerance. When a protocol states that block times average twelve seconds, as Ethereum did before the Merge, users observe confirmations accordingly. When Solana reported high throughput in 2021, developers could measure the consequences: network congestion, forks, and validator restarts during peak loads. Metrics expose truth.

Architecture also reveals responsibility. Developers maintain clients. Validators secure consensus. RPC providers connect wallets. Indexers such as The Graph, launched in December 2020, enable applications to query data efficiently. Each component has a failure mode. Each introduces risk. When users blame a "network outage", architecture helps diagnose which component failed. Was it a client bug, as with Ethereum's Geth incident in August 2021? Was it congestion, as with Solana's repeated halts in September 2021? Or was it an application-layer issue? The architecture provides answers.

A recurring motif in system design is the boundary. Boundaries clarify what a protocol does and does not guarantee. Ethereum's boundary stops at consensus and state execution; it does not govern how wallets manage seed phrases or how exchanges handle customer assets. When the FTX exchange collapsed in November 2022, billions of dollars in client funds vanished. The Ethereum protocol processed withdrawals and transfers exactly as designed. The failure occurred at the edge, where users trusted an institution rather than the protocol. That boundary matters.

Yet boundaries can blur. Many users treat wallet interfaces as part of the protocol. Many assume node providers reflect decentralisation even when a small number of companies relay most traffic.

Architecture diagrams help restore perspective. They reveal that the protocol is the minimal, collectively enforced rule set beneath the stack. Everything above it is software, infrastructure, and governance—not consensus.

Understanding architecture allows us to evaluate claims about scalability, security, or decentralisation with precision. When a protocol claims high throughput, we ask: at what latency? At what validator count? Under what failure conditions? When a system claims to be "trustless", we identify where trust re-enters: in code audits, in human governance, in economic assumptions. When a whitepaper describes a novel consensus mechanism, we examine its safety proofs and liveness guarantees. The question is always the same: what does the architecture actually enforce?

The gulf between hype and architecture will widen as new protocols emerge. Headlines will celebrate breakthroughs. Critics will dismiss them. Markets will react. But beneath the noise, the diagram remains: wallet → node → mempool → validator → state. That chain determines what a system can and cannot do. It is the lens through which meaningful judgment occurs.

One unresolved tension now stands before the reader: when you next encounter a bold claim—whether from a foundation, a start-up, or an excited community—will you accept the painted façade, or will you look through the window and trace how the system truly works?

What Changes, What Stays

At 14:28 UTC on 8 September 2020, the Solana mainnet beta halted. Validators across Frankfurt, Ashburn, and Tokyo stopped producing blocks after an overwhelming burst of automated transactions saturated the queue. Engineers from the Solana Foundation coordinated over Discord in an attempt to restart the network. The event became a touchstone because it exposed a structural truth that marketing cannot soften: no matter how novel a protocol appears, it remains bound by physics, incentives, and human decision-making. Latency cannot be wished away.

Coordination cannot be automated entirely. Behaviour under stress reveals the architecture beneath the narrative.

If one studies distributed systems long enough, the surprise is not that networks fail but that they function at all. A protocol spans continents, expectations, and economic interests. Each participant acts locally. The network behaves globally. Between those layers lies a field of constraints—fixed, measurable, and stubborn. The motif here is a hinge. A hinge determines how two pieces move in relation to one another. It restricts motion even as it enables it. In decentralised systems, constraints act like hinges: they define what can move and what must stay fixed.

The first of these constraints is latency. In April 1998, Google's earliest infrastructure in Stanford's Computer Science building processed queries on a makeshift cluster of commodity machines. Even then, researchers faced the same physical limit: information cannot propagate faster than the speed of light. Today's blockchain networks face this ceiling too. A validator in Sydney receives a block proposal slightly later than one in Paris because the photons must cross oceans. That behaviour is visible: a timestamp lags, a slot misses, a finality checkpoint drifts. No upgrade, no token incentive, no consensus rebrand can compress those milliseconds beyond physics. The implication is immediate. Global agreement is slow by nature. Local computation is fast. Systems that pretend otherwise drift into fantasy.

Ethereum's transition to proof of stake in September 2022 illustrated the same hinge. Beacon chain validators commit attestations every twelve seconds. The design assumes validators can receive, verify, and propagate messages within that interval. If a validator runs on under-provisioned hardware—as many did in early testnets—missed attestations accumulate. The network tolerates this because it prices lateness explicitly: a validator earns less for delayed participation. A protocol that denies latency invites failure. A protocol that measures latency can adapt.

But latency alone does not shape structure. Incentives pull just as strongly. Bitcoin miners in 2013 concentrated operations in China's Sichuan province because hydropower during the rainy season offered ultracheap electricity. This was not ideology; it was arithmetic. The visible behaviour was unmistakable: hash rate surged in the region, and mining pools grew. Decentralisation in theory drifted into concentration in practice. When China banned industrial mining in June 2021, hash power migrated to Kazakhstan and Texas. The protocol had not changed. Human responses to incentives had. The implication is clear. A decentralised system may converge on a centralised geography if incentives align strongly enough.

A counter-example reveals nuance. The Tor network, maintained by The Tor Project since 2006, depends on volunteer-operated relays across dozens of countries. Even with no financial reward, thousands of individuals maintain nodes. The behaviour—steady relay participation—shows that incentives are not always monetary; they can be moral, communal, or political. Yet the limitation remains: participation fluctuates as volunteers' circumstances shift. The network depends on goodwill. That dependence caps capacity. The hinge holds.

The third constraint—human behaviour—may be the least predictable and the most decisive. In March 2022, a group of validators on the Osmosis blockchain coordinated a patch after discovering that a faulty upgrade allowed double-spending. Users rushed to exploit the bug. Developers rushed to stop them. The behaviour is evidence: when rules fail, actors follow their incentives. Human responses expose system weaknesses faster than models predict. No protocol is immune. A system's safety emerges not only from cryptography but from how participants act when incentives collide with ethics.

These constraints—latency, incentives, behaviour—define the range of motion for decentralisation. They turn the binary into a spectrum. A network is not "decentralised" or "centralised"; it is decentralised *at certain layers*, centralised *by certain forces*, and constrained *in specific ways*. Consider DNS, formalised in 1983. It is a decentralised naming system, yet it relies on a small number of root servers operated by known organisations. The architecture distributes authority at lower tiers while concentrating responsibility at the top. This design reflects a judgment about what must stay stable. Stability, not purity, anchors the hinge.

By contrast, peer-to-peer file networks like BitTorrent—released by Bram Cohen in 2001—distribute both authority and operation. Peers exchange pieces of files directly. The behaviour is decentralised by default: a torrent persists as long as even a few peers continue seeding. Yet BitTorrent trackers, which coordinate swarm discovery, became central weaknesses under pressure from law enforcement agencies in the mid-2000s. Even a radically distributed protocol can hinge on a few crucial components. The spectrum narrows.

The central question is not whether decentralisation is desirable. It is which parts of a system must decentralise to preserve the freedoms we seek, and which parts can remain centralised without undermining them. Suppose we examine global consensus—Ethereum's, Bitcoin's, or any other network's. Consensus defines shared state. It must be global because the ledger must be consistent. The cost is slow updates and non-negotiable resource requirements. That is the hinge: global coordination demands friction.

Local caching presents the opposite pattern. A user retrieving a frequently accessed file from a nearby node requires no global coordination. It is faster, cheaper, and safer. Content delivery networks (CDNs), perfected by Akamai from 1999 onward, built their empire on this truth. Even decentralised networks like IPFS mimic the strategy. The principle is simple. Cache what can be cached. Coordinate only when necessary.

Designing a decentralised system is therefore an exercise in identifying which components demand strict agreement and which can tolerate autonomy. Payments? Global. Interface rendering? Local. Identity roots? Shared. Application preferences? Personal. Each choice commits to a trade-off. Each trade-off locks the hinge at a specific angle.

Consider two concrete examples. First, the Bitcoin mempool. Each node maintains its own queue of pending transactions. No protocol mandates global mempool synchronisation. Nodes vary in what they accept, reject, or prioritise based on fee thresholds. This local autonomy reduces bandwidth requirements and allows the network to tolerate regional partitioning. Behaviour diverges. The chain converges. The hinge balances independence and agreement.

Second, the Filecoin retrieval market, launched in October 2020. Storage providers commit evidence to the chain to prove they hold data over time. Retrieval, however, does not require global consensus. A client requests data directly from providers. This division reflects a clear principle. Verification is global. Transfer is local. A system that attempted to achieve global consensus on every retrieval would collapse under its own weight. The hinge keeps the motion constrained.

If decentralisation is a spectrum, where should the slider sit? That depends on what the system protects. When a ledger determines financial balances, we commit to global verification. When a user opens an application, we rely on local rendering. When a smart contract changes the rules of a network, we require collective agreement. When a user toggles a setting in their wallet, we respect personal control. These distinctions are behavioural, not philosophical. They describe who must trust whom, and when.

A limitation demonstrates the boundary. Fully decentralised messaging systems like Secure Scuttlebutt, created by Dominic Tarr in 2014, allow users to store and replicate social feeds without a server. But they struggle with device switching and onboarding because identity is tied to a specific device's key. The decentralisation is authentic. The user experience suffers. The hinge restricts motion. The implication is unavoidable. Some tasks—sync, recovery, spam control—benefit from structured coordination.

The spectrum becomes visible in the wild behaviour of systems under load. Ethereum gas prices during the NFT surge of August 2021 spiked above 300 gwei. Users complained. Developers adjusted contracts. Wallets implemented gas estimators. A global, scarce resource—block space—created friction precisely because it is shared. Local caching could not solve it. The hinge had reached its limit. The constraint held.

If these constraints seem restrictive, it is because we rarely acknowledge that decentralised architectures are not blank canvases.

They are mechanical assemblies shaped by limits. The artistry lies in arranging these limits to preserve autonomy without sacrificing usability. Too much coordination suffocates participation. Too little coordination fragments the network. The hinge must hold without binding too tightly.

One final question remains. As new systems emerge—identity layers, storage networks, federated governance models—how will we determine which components deserve global coordination and which must remain local? The answer cannot be abstract. It must be measured in latency budgets, observed incentives, and human behaviour under strain. What must change? What must stay?

Chapter 2
Owning the Web

The moment feels trivial. You download a new app, keen to explore whatever service or distraction it promises, and are met with the familiar ritual: create an account, set a password, verify your email, agree to terms you will never read. Some apps allow you to reuse a login from a social platform, but that convenience hides a deep dependency: your identity online belongs to someone else. If that platform decides to revoke access, or simply cease to exist, your ability to prove who you are vanishes with it. The keys to your digital life sit on a shelf you do not own.

Ownership in the physical world is simple. If you hold the keys to your house, you control who enters. If you buy a book, you may lend it, annotate it, or leave it to a friend. Online, the relationship is murkier. You can purchase a film, but the studio may remove it from your library without notice. You can store thousands of photos in a cloud service, yet lose them if a password reset fails or a billing card expires. We call these possessions, but the control they confer is conditional. Our digital belongings behave more like rented privileges than property. We live in a world where owning the web feels increasingly like an illusion.

At the heart of this chapter lies a question that modern life seldom pauses to ask: what does it mean to truly own something online? The paradox is jarring. Our identities, data, memories, and relationships are more digital than ever, yet our authority over them has never been more fragile. A forgotten password can invalidate a lifetime of evidence. A change to a privacy policy can redefine who sees the most intimate details of our existence. A corporate merger can suddenly relocate our past into servers in another jurisdiction. Ownership, once a simple lock and key, now resembles a shifting negotiation.

The decentralised web proposes an alternative: ownership not as a legal fiction enforced by corporate discretion, but as a set of cryptographically enforceable rights held directly by individuals. Identity becomes self-sovereign, not merely self-declared. Data becomes portable, not trapped. Assets become transferable and persist beyond the lifespan of the platforms that support them. In this future, the architecture of power changes. You do not ask permission to participate; you carry your credentials with you. You do not seek an export link buried in settings; your data follows your decisions. You do not hope a customer support representative understands your situation; you hold the keys.

Yet genuine ownership carries responsibilities. A wallet controlled solely by its owner places the burden of recovery on the human behind the device. Multisignature policies can spread risk across trusted guardians—a family member, a lawyer, a friend—but that trust must be chosen carefully. The same cryptography that makes censorship difficult also makes mistakes irreversible. A lost key is not an inconvenience; it is an erasure. For all its promise, autonomy can be frighteningly lonely.

This is not a new tension. Property rights have always balanced independence with protection. A home provides shelter but requires maintenance. A bank account grants access to money but depends on institutional safeguards. The digital age merely adds new layers. Who inherits a father's cryptocurrency when he passes away? Who accesses the health records of an incapacitated patient if the credentials are locked behind biometric authentication? These are human concerns dressed in unfamiliar technical clothing. They remind us that digital ownership must coexist with mortality, forgetfulness, trust, and care.

Self-sovereign identity offers a glimpse of freedom from the repetitive bureaucracy of the web. One decentralised identifier—your DID—could authenticate you to dozens of services without repeatedly handing over your name, birthday, and entire address book. Verifiable credentials could prove you are a student, a homeowner, or over eighteen without exposing unnecessary information. The act of proving becomes selective, not extractive. Instead of leaving breadcrumbs of personal detail on every site you visit, you carry a privacy-preserving credential in your wallet—cryptographic, portable, and controlled by you.

But for this model to flourish, services must do more than export data. They must accept imported identity and records without suspicion or penalty. Imagine moving your music library from one streaming service to another without losing curated playlists painstakingly assembled over years. Or bringing your professional profile to a new workplace app without retyping your employment history—a stack of verifiable credentials proving exactly what needs to be proved. The technology exists, but incentives lag. Portability threatens monopolies built on captivity. Openness is rarely in the business model of incumbents.

Digital ownership cannot remain a privilege reserved for those who understand cryptography. It must become a foundation accessible to everyone. That means designing systems resilient not only against attackers but against everyday life: lost phones, forgotten PINs, changing family structures, devices shared by partners or siblings. A system that collapses when a human errs is not a system that serves humans. Recovery must be engineered into ownership without reintroducing old gatekeepers.

One motif will surface repeatedly in this chapter: control across contexts. True ownership means authority persists even when the environment changes. If you move house, your physical possessions follow. If you change service providers, your digital possessions should too. The web today breaks this principle. Your photos live inside one app's database. Your professional network exists inside another. Your education credentials float in yet another system, inaccessible without passwords or mutual trust agreements. Centralisation creates convenience until convenience becomes captivity.

The decentralised alternative does not imply abandoning all institutions. Rather, it proposes that institutions recognise users as peers rather than dependencies. A bank could hold digital assets without owning them. A healthcare provider could store encrypted records without accessing them. A social network could become a client rather than a container, competing on experience rather than enclosure. Control shifts outward, to the edges of the network where people live their digital lives.

Owning the web is not about speculative assets or technological bravado. It is about dignity. It is about ensuring that the digital mirror which reflects our lives cannot be taken from us, weaponised against us, or lost to a glitch in a system we do not govern. It is about ensuring that children who grow up entirely online inherit something more resilient than a portfolio of accounts and recoverable usernames. It is about acknowledging that the web is now part of who we are—and designing rights that honour that truth.

This chapter will confront uncomfortable trade-offs. It will examine what individuals should truly control and where shared infrastructure better serves community safety. It will ask how we create systems that empower the vulnerable rather than burden them. It will challenge the assumption that more control always equals better outcomes. Ownership is not a single switch to flip; it is a set of choices about when to delegate, when to verify, and when to trust.

We are connected by accounts we do not own, protected by passwords we forget, and shaped by data we cannot inspect. The decentralised web invites us to change that—to build a digital home where the door belongs to us, not the landlord. But rights without responsibility are fragile. And autonomy without support is a myth.

As we explore identity, data, property, and custody in the sections ahead, a question will accompany us: when you close the laptop and walk away, who remains in control of your digital life—you, or the systems that watch over it?

Self-sovereign Identity

In September 2021, LinkedIn briefly locked out millions of users in the United Kingdom after an automated security system flagged suspected "unusual activity". People who had built careers, found jobs, and maintained professional reputations through that platform discovered that they could not even view their own profiles. Every attempt to appeal or authenticate redirected them to a form controlled entirely by the company. The outcome was mundane yet unsettling: individuals temporarily lost their professional identities because a remote process judged them incorrectly. The event revealed a quiet truth. Identity online is often borrowed, not owned.

How did we arrive at a digital world where proving who we are depends on passwords, captchas, and the goodwill of platforms? The mechanism is visible. Each sign-up demands familiar behaviour: enter personal details, create a credential, verify through another digital gatekeeper. It is repetitive, extractive, and fundamentally centralised. Over 70% of internet users abandon at least one application a year due to login friction, according to a 2020 FIDO Alliance report. The friction accumulates into fatigue. We duplicate fragments of ourselves across hundreds of forms. A question lingers in the background like a quiet motif: who owns the act of identification?

Self-sovereign identity (SSI) reframes the answer. Instead of being granted by companies, identity becomes something individuals create and carry. A decentralised identifier (DID) operates as a stable anchor—not an account in a corporate database but a cryptographic pointer controlled by a person. Verifiable credentials turn claims into proofs: a university can issue a digital diploma that you can present anywhere without giving the issuer perpetual oversight. A wallet—software or hardware—becomes the personal vault where these credentials live. The shift is subtle and structural. Authority moves from centre to edge.

Show the difference, then name it. Today, if you wish to sign into government services in Estonia, the Smart-ID system—launched nationwide in 2017—allows citizens to authenticate with a digital identity stored securely on their devices, recognised across banking, healthcare, and bureaucratic systems. The user presents a self-held credential. The verifier trusts the signature, not the platform. The implication is striking. One identity unlocks the state.

Contrast this with a typical US-based social media login. A "Sign in with Facebook" button removes friction, but only by introducing dependency. If Facebook suspends an account—as happened to journalist Nandini Jammi in 2019 during an automated moderation sweep—applications tied to that login collapse. Trust is abstract until behaviour exposes its edges. A dependency becomes visible only when it breaks.

SSI advocates argue that identity should resemble a set of keys, not a single gate. Each credential functions independently. A driving licence does not rely on your supermarket loyalty account. Yet digital systems routinely entangle unrelated fragments of life because companies benefit from aggregation. When a bank demands access to your phone number and email and social profile to reset a password, convenience masks extraction. A verified claim becomes an oversight channel.

Portable identity offers a counter-behaviour. Imagine using the same DID to log into a budgeting service, a job portal, and a social forum. You present only the necessary proofs. No re-registration. No handing away your contacts list. Authentication shifts from interrogation to permission. That is self-sovereignty expressed through routine action.

But portability introduces new risks. If a single private key unlocks your digital life, loss becomes catastrophic. In January 2021, The New York Times reported that German programmer Stefan Thomas could not access 7,002 bitcoins because he had lost the key to his hardware wallet. The wealth existed mathematically; it was inaccessible practically. A forgotten password locked away a fortune. The limitation becomes ethics: autonomy without safety creates brittle power.

Recovery systems must therefore evolve. Social guardianship—first formalised in the Web3 space through projects like Argent's wallet (launched 2020)—allows trusted people or institutions to approve key resets without holding the key themselves. It mirrors a familiar social behaviour: we give spare house keys to family or neighbours in case of trouble. This design recognises that humans misplace things, relationships shift, and emergencies happen. But it also reveals an implication. Trust re-enters through people, not protocols. No architecture fully eliminates dependency; it merely chooses where to place it.

Two more examples clarify the stakes. In 2023, the city of Zug in Switzerland expanded its eID project so residents could use decentralised identifiers to access local services. A resident can present a verifiable credential proving residency without exposing full personal histories. Behaviour becomes precise: prove exactly what needs proving, nothing more. Meanwhile, refugees fleeing conflict zones—from Syria in the mid-2010s to Ukraine in 2022—often lose paper documents and rely on fragile bureaucracies for recognition. A portable digital credential could preserve rights across borders when physical documents fail. Identity becomes a companion rather than a tether.

The motif of ownership resurfaces here. To own identity is to carry authority wherever you go. But authority is not static. A credential loses validity when the issuer revokes it, just as a passport expires. Sovereignty does not eliminate dependence on institutions; it balances it. The challenge lies in governance. Who defines the rules for revocation? Who arbitrates disputes? Self-sovereignty is not isolation. It is negotiation with new leverage.

Critics underline a counter-example worth engaging. Centralised identity providers can respond quickly to fraud. If someone compromises a Google account, automated systems detect anomalies within minutes due to behavioural analytics at scale. A decentralised wallet cannot easily revoke a compromised key. Without careful planning, autonomy could weaken security. This tension demands design that prioritises safe defaults: hardware isolation of keys, staged approvals for sensitive actions, and community-based recourse mechanisms. Cryptography may secure credentials; communities secure people.

The question then becomes not *whether* self-sovereign identity should replace existing systems, but *where* it offers more dignity and resilience. It excels when proof must travel across contexts: employment, education, residency, credentials crossing jurisdictions. It struggles when individuals face deep vulnerabilities: cognitive impairment, coercion, digital illiteracy. A hinge metaphor fits: SSI enables movement but must not allow the structure to collapse when pressed.

Zoom in once more to the everyday action. A person in Manchester signs into a new budgeting app using a DID controlled through a wallet on their phone. They approve a selective disclosure: proof of income bracket without exposing employer details. The app verifies a cryptographic signature anchored on a public ledger, not by querying a social platform's API. The identity event belongs to the user. Should the app misbehave or decline, the DID remains intact. A door opens without a key changing hands.

Zoom out again to society. A future where people own identity could reduce the surveillance incentives embedded into central sign-in systems. Advertising giants would lose the choke-point through which they currently observe login behaviour across the internet. Service providers might compete on user experience rather than data capture. Regulatory compliance could become demonstrable through verifiable proofs rather than bulk data transfers vulnerable to breach. The implications ripple outward. Rights gain implementation.

Yet the unresolved tension persists like a quiet question under every paragraph: how much responsibility should an ordinary person bear for securing the core of their digital existence? Too much burden leads to loss. Too little leads to dependency. The hinge must hold.

Self-sovereign identity points towards a digital world where recognition is not conditional on corporate approval, where credentials endure beyond platform lifespans, and where individuals participate as principals rather than products. But it asks something demanding in return: assume authority for yourself. Protect it. Maintain it. Choose your guardians wisely.

When control sits in your hand, the risk sits there too. So does the opportunity. The next time you click "Create account", what would it mean to bring your identity with you rather than surrendering it anew?

Data Portability in Practice

In January 2019, a small Dublin-based company called Soundiiz announced that it had helped users migrate over one billion music tracks between streaming platforms. A person could move a playlist crafted over years from Spotify to Apple Music—or to Deezer, Pandora, or Tidal—without rebuilding it song by song. Yet the celebration came with a caveat. Behind every successful transfer was a meticulous technical dance: matching track identifiers across catalogues that do not agree on metadata, handling duplicates, interpreting regional licensing differences. When Spotify removed a track from its catalogue, the receiving service often displayed a gap—an empty slot where memory should be. The scene illustrated a truth that rarely enters public view: data portability is not a switch, but a fragile choreography of formats, incentives, and human patience.

The motif here is a suitcase. A suitcase protects personal belongings as we move through life. We expect to pack it, carry it, open it anywhere. On the web, the suitcase often arrives locked by someone else's key. That mismatch—possession without portability—defines the modern data experience.

Show the tension, then name it. The General Data Protection Regulation (GDPR), enforced in the European Union since May 2018, codified the right to data portability in Article 20. Companies must allow individuals to export their personal data "in a structured, commonly used and machine-readable format." This sounds straightforward. But the behaviour users encounter—CSV dumps, JSON blobs, zipped archives containing obscure folder structures—reveals that "machine-readable" does not guarantee *interoperable*. A suitcase full of belongings is only useful if the next place accepts what is inside.

Formats shape outcomes. When a user exports their photos from Google Takeout, launched in 2011, they receive thousands of image files accompanied by JSON metadata about timestamps, locations, and albums. Importing those photos into Apple Photos in London in 2023 preserves the images but discards many contextual details. The schema differs. The photo moves. The meaning weakens. The implication is clear. Without shared semantics, portability becomes a half-truth: you carry the file but lose the story.

Music streaming makes the paradox visible. Services store playlists as ordered references to catalogue identifiers. A track might exist under different ISRC codes in different regions. Soundiiz and competitors like FreeYourMusic must guess equivalences. A match succeeds. A cherished live version disappears. The user blames the intermediary. The root cause is the asymmetry of power. Catalogues are proprietary. Schemas diverge. The suitcase arrives dented.

Systems can do better. In the academic world, ORCID identifiers—widely adopted since 2012—allow researchers to maintain a persistent identity across publishers and institutions. When an article is published in Elsevier's system in Amsterdam or archived by arXiv in New York, the attribution attaches to the same global identifier. The behaviour is elegant: update once, propagate everywhere. The implication is significant. Standardisation enables portability that does not depend on negotiations between competitors.

But incentives govern adoption. Why would an incumbent platform, whose business thrives on exclusive engagement, make exit easier? When WhatsApp launched encrypted backups in 2021, migration to competing messengers remained cumbersome. Conversations are entangled with phone numbers, device identifiers, and proprietary formats. Lock-in is deliberate. Companies measure retention as a growth metric. They resist anything that erodes that moat. Portability threatens business models built on captivity.

There is a credible counter-example that complicates the picture. Email, formalised through SMTP in 1982, permits full migration of messages via IMAP or POP. A user can switch providers without losing correspondence. Yet Gmail maintains overwhelming dominance. This persistence shows that portability alone does not guarantee movement. Convenience, spam filtering, and search quality anchor behaviour. The suitcase moves easily. People choose not to move. The limitation reminds us that technical possibility must meet human motivation.

Still, friction hurts. The Data Transfer Project—an initiative led by Google, Microsoft, Meta, and Twitter since 2018—aims to automate export/import pipelines. A user should be able to migrate photos from Facebook to Google Photos without downloading anything locally. The behaviour appears seamless. But progress is uneven, and APIs impose subtle restrictions: rate limits, missing fields, inconsistent error handling. A suitcase with wheels still catches on cracks. The implication is unavoidable. Portability that depends on corporate goodwill can be revoked as quickly as it is granted.

Versioning complicates matters further. When Slack modifies its data schema, export archives from 2020 may not import cleanly into a future platform without transformation. Names change. Fields deprecate. Attachments shift storage layers. Version history becomes as important as data itself. A portable suitcase requires a map of how its contents evolved. Without that, interoperability decays over time.

User experience remains the quiet determinant of success. Imagine a family in Birmingham exporting its media library from Netflix after a decade of viewing. They discover that their viewing history cannot be imported elsewhere, that "My List" becomes a plaintext file, that personalised recommendations evaporate. The portable archive feels hollow. The suitcase travelled, but the sentiment stayed behind. Memory is portable only when context travels with it.

A more promising pattern emerges in decentralised storage networks. IPFS, originally released by Protocol Labs in 2015, identifies files by cryptographic hash. If two services store the same file, they reference the same identifier. The suitcase metaphor shifts. Instead of carrying possessions everywhere, you carry proofs of possession. Data persists anywhere a node chooses to store it. Yet the limitation is again behavioural. If no one pins the data, the content becomes unreachable despite the identifier persisting. Portability requires stewardship. The hinge holds.

Portability also intersects with rights. Health records in the United Kingdom can be downloaded via NHS login, but those records often remain unreadable by third-party applications due to inconsistent FHIR implementation. The behaviour is revealing: patients have export rights, but the healthcare ecosystem is slow to accept imports.

A suitcase cannot enter the building. Until acceptance becomes as mandatory as export, rights remain abstract.

The recurring question—threaded quietly through this narrative—is not simply *can* users take their data with them? It is *will* the next service recognise and respect it? A system that only supports outbound movement reinforces central power. A system that embraces inbound understanding redistributes agency.

Show the stakes. When a young artist in Lagos migrates from Instagram to a decentralised social platform, they want their followers, captions, and creative history to come along. When a professional in Edinburgh leaves a dying SaaS product, they want to retain the workflow structures they built. When a teenager in Brighton switches phones after an accident, they want their chats and photos restored without bureaucratic hassle. The suitcase should always open. The belongings should still make sense.

What would real portability look like? A file format like JPEG (established 1992) succeeded because any camera could produce it and any viewer could display it. A contact record like vCard (1996) works across systems because fields map predictably. To advance, web services need similar commitments: schemas governed by open standards, version histories machine-readable, mapping tables maintained by both sides of a transfer. Portability requires common language, not just access privileges.

Incentives must shift. Platforms could gain goodwill by advertising "easy exit" as a mark of confidence. Regulators could mandate interoperability checks before data-intensive services launch. Users could choose products that treat their data as something worth keeping elsewhere. Competition should occur at the level of service quality, not data captivity.

Yet a tension remains unresolved: how do we ensure that portable data does not become portable surveillance? A contact list stored in your wallet is powerful; a compromised wallet becomes catastrophic. A health record that moves easily could be misused if protections weaken across borders. The suitcase must be secure even as it becomes mobile.

The final question lingers: when the next service offers to store your memories, will it treat your data as luggage you own or property you rent?

Property without Possession

On 17 July 2009, Amazon remotely deleted copies of George Orwell's *1984* from Kindles across the United States after discovering that a third-party seller lacked the rights to distribute the ebook. Readers awoke to find a title they had purchased simply gone. Refunds arrived automatically, yet the shock lingered: a possession had vanished without consent, without warning, and without recourse. The event revealed an unsettling asymmetry. In the digital realm, owning something does not always mean being able to keep it.

The motif threading through this chapter is a lock. A lock promises security but also enforces dependency. Whoever holds the master key decides what "ownership" means. In physical life, that is straightforward. In digital life, the master key often resides elsewhere.

Show the mechanism, then name it. Digital ownership is rarely a single right. It is a bundle: access, reproduction, modification, distribution, duration. Companies such as Apple, Google, and Amazon sell digital goods in marketplaces governed by licences rather than classical property law. A film purchased on iTunes in London in 2020 can disappear when licensing agreements change, even if you paid full price. A book downloaded on Kindle might become inaccessible if your account is suspended. The behaviour is visible in every "Buy" button tied to a terms-of-service document: possession is conditional, revocable.

Now consider a more intimate case: a personal photo library. A family in Glasgow stores tens of thousands of images on Google Photos. These images document births, funerals, friendships, first days at school. The files feel like property—emotional, personal, irreplaceable. But what the family actually "owns" is a licence to store and access photographs on Google's servers, governed by policies updated unilaterally. If they export the data, the JPEGs travel, but the albums, labels, and face clustering—structures built by proprietary machine-learning models—do not. The file moves, the meaning thins. The implication is clear. Possession without context is not ownership.

Another named example clarifies scope. In October 2022, Meta began integrating its Accounts Center across Facebook and Instagram, allowing unified login management. This simplification made switching accounts easier but also increased the risk that suspension of one account could cascade across others. A person who loses access to Instagram might suddenly find their Facebook Marketplace listings or saved memories unreachable. A single decision by a platform becomes a multi-domain lock. The user's assets depend on corporate adjudication, not personal authority.

Ownership should instead mean enforceable control across contexts. That principle extends beyond files. Take domain names. When a business in Brighton registers a .uk domain through Nominet, it does not "own" the string outright; it leases it under strict terms. If the renewal fee is missed or compliance falters, the domain can be revoked and resold. Yet a domain name behaves like property in that it grants recognisable authority anchored by DNS. This blend of rights—time-bounded, conditional, but transferable—illustrates the ambiguity. Digital resources live in a space between licence and property, their security shaped by institutions rather than place.

A counter-example shows what durable ownership can look like. In the realm of decentralised file networks, Arweave—launched in 2018 with headquarters originally in London—offers permanent data storage backed by a cryptographic protocol and long-term economic model. Once uploaded, data is intended to persist indefinitely as long as miners continue to participate. A user cannot be unilaterally locked out by a central authority; the protocol enforces access via public keys. Yet even here, the promise is partial. If the user loses their private key, retrieval becomes impossible. Permanence exists only if the owner maintains their side of the lock. The limitation reinforces a broader truth. Digital ownership requires stewardship.

Access control defines ownership in practice. Whoever decides who enters and who is excluded holds real power. Cloud platforms operate access control as policy. You log in, your credentials are verified, and the system grants entry. But the platform—Amazon, Microsoft, Dropbox—determines the threshold. A misconfigured security setting can lock you out of your own documents. A billing failure can suspend your files. A content-moderation ruling can erase years of work. These actions reflect institutional priorities, not necessarily the intentions of the person creating the data.

The distinction between licensing and owning becomes especially visible when a service terminates. When Google ended its Picasa Web Albums product in 2016, users could export their images but not the organisational ecosystem they had built—shared albums, captions, nested collections. When Nintendo shut down the Wii Shop Channel in 2019, customers permanently lost access to purchased games unless they had downloaded them locally. The behaviour is undeniable: files exist only within the scaffolding of platforms. Remove the platform, and the asset collapses into fragments.

Yet there are instructive models that honour continuity. The Creative Commons licences, introduced in 2002, provide predictable bundles of rights for creative works that travel across platforms. When a photographer in Leeds releases a photo under CC-BY, any service—Flickr, Wikimedia, personal websites—can reuse it as long as attribution is preserved. The licence attaches to the work, not the platform. The control is portable. This approach demonstrates that ownership can be framed around obligations and freedoms rather than corporate terms.

Transferability is another hinge. Physical property changes hands through sale, gift, or inheritance. Digital assets, however, often resist transfer. An ebook cannot be resold legally under the standard Kindle licence. A purchased online game might be tied permanently to a specific account. Even a film "owned" on a digital platform cannot be gifted. These restrictions reveal the underlying truth: companies treat digital assets as rented access, not possessions.

But decentralised systems show that other patterns are possible. A non-fungible token (NFT), despite speculative excesses, demonstrates a technical reality: a digital token with a unique identifier can be transferred from one person to another without platform approval. Whether that token points to a meaningful asset is a separate issue, but the act of transfer illustrates that ownership rights can be encoded directly in infrastructure. Yet even here, the limitation surfaces: if the artwork behind the NFT is stored on a private server, the token persists while the image vanishes. The lock works; the door leads nowhere.

Returning to the photo library, the question becomes sharper. What does it mean to *own* a memory that is digitally stored? If the underlying file is a JPEG, you can copy it, store it locally, and back it up in multiple places. But the structure of your library—the albums, tags, facial clusters—is not yours. These are derivative works created by a service's proprietary systems. Migrating to another provider means losing organisational metadata. The lock protects the photo. The latch on the meaning remains controlled elsewhere.

Ownership, then, must be defined not as possessing the file but as retaining enforceable control across contexts: the ability to move, duplicate, delegate, and withdraw without losing value in translation. A right that dissolves when you change platform is not ownership; it is tenancy.

The stakes rise when we consider digital legacies. If a person in Manchester passes away, their heirs may struggle to access cloud-stored photos because the account is bound to authentication factors held only by the deceased. Companies vary in their policies. Apple introduced Digital Legacy in 2021, allowing appointed contacts to request access. Google offers Inactive Account Manager. But these remain privileges granted by platforms, not rights held by individuals. Authority must be sought, not presumed. The master key is not in the family's hands.

A final question settles uneasily at the edge of the narrative: if digital ownership depends on locks we do not control, what changes must we demand so that the memories, creations, and assets we cherish remain ours even when platforms shift, licences expire, or accounts go dark?

Custody, Keys, and Recovery

In August 2013, James Howells of Newport, Wales, accidentally threw away a hard drive containing the private keys to 7,500 Bitcoin. The drive ended up in the municipal landfill. Despite repeated attempts to persuade the council to let him excavate the site, the device remained buried beneath thousands of tonnes of compacted waste. The coins were unrecoverable. No support line, no administrator, no appeals process. A single disk had held the only credential capable of exercising control. Lose it, and the door locked forever. That stark finality captures both the promise and peril of digital self-custody.

A lock appears here again, quiet but insistent. A lock protects; a lock isolates. A lock remembers nothing about your intentions. Its logic is mechanical, indifferent. The possession of a key defines the boundary between control and exclusion. Digital systems intensify this condition. A private key is not an object you can feel. It is a few dozen characters that map directly to authority. Whoever holds it acts. Whoever loses it waits.

Self-custody became a defining ideal of decentralised systems because it inverts the Web2 relationship between users and platforms. Instead of accounts controlled by institutions, authority sits with individuals. Name the relationship for what it is: a transfer of responsibility from corporate systems to human memory, human process, human fallibility. This shift is not a slogan. It is a structural reallocation of risk. The implications stretch across years, families, jurisdictions, and devices.

To see the mechanics, consider hardware wallets such as Ledger, founded in Paris in 2014, or Trezor, first released in Prague in 2013. These devices protect private keys by isolating them from general-purpose computers. When you sign a transaction, the wallet displays the details on a small screen, asking for physical confirmation. The behaviour is visible: a tactile click, a visible prompt, a conscious act.

The security model works because even if your laptop is compromised, the attacker cannot sign on your behalf. Yet the limitation reveals itself quickly. If you lose the wallet and the seed phrase, recovery becomes impossible. Hardware protects keys but does not replace stewardship.

A second named example shows a different pattern. In 2021, the Ethereum Foundation highlighted the growing use of multisignature wallets via Gnosis Safe (now Safe Global) as a governance standard. A multisig requires a threshold—say, three of five authorised signers—to approve transactions. The system is both technical and social. It reduces single points of failure, distributes decision-making, and creates continuity when one device or signer is lost. But the behaviour it enforces has trade-offs. Coordination slows. Responsibilities must be explicit. The group must maintain situational awareness. A multisig reduces individual risk by increasing collective discipline.

Now introduce the counter-example: custodial services. When a user stores assets on a centralised exchange such as Coinbase, founded in San Francisco in 2012, they delegate the entire custody function. The exchange manages private keys, handles backups, resets access, and provides human support. The visible behaviour is familiar: forgotten passwords can be reset via email; disputes can be escalated; assets are recoverable if you misplace your credentials. Yet this ease comes with vulnerability. In 2014, Mt. Gox collapsed in Tokyo after losing approximately 850,000 Bitcoin. Customers who trusted the platform bore the consequences of its internal failures. The lock was held by someone else. When they faltered, the door fell open.

Reconciliation requires nuance. Managed custody is not a moral failure; self-custody is not a universal ideal. Each model expresses a different balance between autonomy and delegation. The real question is where you want the burden of recovery to fall when something goes wrong.

Recovery shapes every other decision. A private key is a single point of authority. If it is compromised, an attacker can drain assets within seconds. If it is lost, your assets may remain inaccessible forever. The stakes demand processes that integrate both cryptography and human practice. Social recovery emerged to bridge the gap. In 2020, Ethereum researcher Vitalik Buterin described a model where guardians—trusted individuals or devices—combine signatures to regenerate a lost key. The behaviour resembles community rituals: recovery becomes an act involving witnesses, not a solitary struggle. Yet the model's strength is also its vulnerability. Guardians must be trustworthy, available, and diverse enough to prevent collusion. The lock becomes a network of locks; the key a collective artefact.

The motif of the lock surfaces again in family settings. Imagine a household in Edinburgh that manages shared digital assets—a savings pool, a set of subscription credentials, a collection of encrypted documents. A single private key would impose unreasonable risk. Instead, they adopt a 2-of-3 multisig policy: one key stored on a hardware wallet, one on a phone-based secure enclave, one held by a guardian outside the household. When a parent dies, the surviving members can still access the assets. When a device breaks, recovery is possible. The lock remains strict, but the path to opening it adapts to human contingencies.

This interplay between human life and cryptographic structure becomes clearest when death enters the frame. A will in the United Kingdom must name beneficiaries and executors, but it cannot meaningfully reference a private key without risking exposure. Families struggle with this tension. If the key is stored too openly, it may be misused. If it is concealed too well, heirs may never retrieve the assets. Some turn to time-locked multisigs; others use sealed envelopes stored with solicitors; others involve digital legacy services. All of these behaviours share one theme: the search for a lock that preserves autonomy during life and continuity after it.

Shared devices complicate matters further. A phone used by multiple family members, a laptop borrowed by a partner, a tablet shared with children—each action widens the attack surface. A moment of inattention can store a seed phrase in an insecure photo album. A well-meaning family member might attempt a recovery process incorrectly. Human behaviour introduces variability that cryptography alone cannot mitigate. The system must fit the rhythms of home life, not merely the threat models of experts.

The tension deepens when we consider institutional contexts. A small charity in Bristol uses a multisig to manage its treasury. Trustees rotate every two years. Devices change. People move, fall ill, or resign unexpectedly. Without precise onboarding and offboarding procedures, keys drift out of sync with reality. The charity risks loss not due to hackers but due to organisational entropy. The lock becomes misaligned with the people meant to open it.

A second example sharpens the point. In 2022, the Ukrainian government used multi-party signing across ministries to distribute emergency funds during the early invasion months. The structure prevented unilateral misappropriation while ensuring rapid deployment. The multisig provided resilience amid crisis. Yet it required continuous coordination: officials had to be reachable; communication lines had to remain stable. Even the most secure architecture depends on the availability and coherence of the humans operating it.

The counterpoint appears in custodial models tailored for inheritance. Some wealth managers now offer key escrow services under regulated frameworks. If a client storing cryptographic assets in Zurich dies, the service can release access to heirs through legal processes. The behaviour mirrors traditional financial custodianship. Yet it sacrifices confidentiality and sovereign control. The company becomes the master key. If compromised, coerced, or insolvent, the assets become vulnerable. Delegation solves one problem by creating another.

The quiet motif—this question of the lock—threads through every scenario. Where is the lock? Who controls the key? How many doors must open for the system to function? The friction emerges because digital authority is absolute. A metal key can be copied, a lock replaced, a door forced in emergencies. A cryptographic key has no physical weak point. It cannot be guessed, duplicated, or bypassed. That strength is also its severity.

The technical choices reflect this. Hardware wallets commit to physical separation. Multisigs commit to threshold consensus. Social recovery commits to a web of trust anchored by human judgement.

Custodial services commit to institutional processes. Each option measures its trade-offs differently: security versus convenience, autonomy versus support, resilience versus complexity. None of these choices are neutral.

The decision becomes most vivid when loss hovers. Imagine the moment after a phone falls from a balcony or a laptop is stolen from a café in Leeds. The user must ask: what is the failure mode? If the key lives solely on the device, the assets are at risk or lost. If the seed phrase is written in a rarely visited drawer, retrieval might take hours. If the key is distributed across guardians, coordination becomes essential. The architecture reveals itself not in diagrams but in stress.

This raises the forward question the chapter cannot evade: if the lock defines ownership, and the key defines authority, how do we design custody systems that honour human lives—messy, mortal, collaborative—without compromising the cryptographic guarantees that give decentralised systems their strength?

Chapter 3
Trust Without Gatekeepers

On 15 August 1971, President Richard Nixon announced that the United States would no longer allow the dollar to be exchanged for gold. For decades, the global monetary system had derived its credibility from convertibility into a precious metal that no single government controlled. Nixon's announcement severed that anchor. Overnight, the world's financial order became a consensus system. Money continued to function not because it was backed by anything tangible, but because everyone agreed—reluctantly or otherwise—to keep playing the game. The moment marked a shift from trust in metal to trust in institutions, from physics to promises. Yet promises can fray.

Half a century later, digital networks expose the same tension at far greater scale. We now move billions of pounds daily through systems that rely on shared belief rather than shared custody. Visa approves a payment not because it sees a pile of banknotes but because its ledgers align with a bank's ledgers and regulators trust the banks. Fraud is handled later. Trust is assumed upfront. It works—until it doesn't. A hacked card. A frozen account. A disputed transaction. Human intermediaries step in, investigate, adjudicate. They wield authority because we allow them to. They arbitrate because the architecture depends on it.

But what if trust could be engineered differently? What if we could coordinate action among strangers without appointing anyone as the final arbiter of truth? What if rules could be enforced by mathematics rather than gatekeepers? These are not merely technical questions. They shape power: who controls economic flows, who can be silenced, who can be surveilled, who can be excluded.

Decentralised systems promise a world where participants reach agreement without deferring to a single judge. They do so by making deceit expensive and honesty rewarding. That shift—from trusting people to trusting incentives and code—rearranges old assumptions. Instead of architecture built around central offices, we have networks in which each participant verifies their peers. Instead of passwords stored by companies, we have cryptographic signatures owned by individuals. Instead of appeals processes and customer support hotlines, we have finality: once recorded, certain actions cannot be reversed.

The stakes become clearest when money enters the frame. Blockchains emerged not from abstract curiosity but from a failure of trust after the 2008 financial crisis. Banks had gambled with depositors' funds, then relied on governments to absorb losses. Centralised trust had proven brittle and political. In response, engineers sought to design a monetary network where *no* institution could unilaterally change the rules. The architecture encoded a principle: if you validate the work, you earn the right to secure the system. Proof-of-work was both a computational lottery and a political statement.

Yet the method of reaching agreement is never neutral. Proof-of-work ties influence to energy expenditure; proof-of-stake ties it to wealth at stake; smaller committee-based systems tie it to selected validators. Each approach embodies a philosophy. Each carries distinct vulnerabilities. There is no perfect consensus, only trade-offs: speed versus decentralisation, efficiency versus openness, safety versus flexibility. Readers will find that arguments about "the best system" often mask disagreements about whose power should be privileged.

If consensus defines how networks trust themselves, incentives define how they protect themselves. A system survives only if honest participation pays better than cheating. That simple rule hides a web of complications. A spam attack on a blockchain's transaction queue—its mempool—may not seek financial gain at all; it may attempt to stall progress, censor opponents, or cause reputational damage. Security becomes an optimisation problem with adversaries who do not behave like neat rational agents in economics textbooks. Good design imagines the worst behaviour and prices it out of reach.

Then comes the problem of the world beyond the network. Blockchains excel at agreeing on the state of their own ledgers. They struggle when they must depend on external facts: the price of a currency, the result of an election, the honesty of a data feed. The code is definitive but blind. Between smart contracts and reality lies an oracle: a mechanism that brings outside truth in. When oracles fail—through bugs, manipulation, or ambiguity—code can execute with ruthless consistency while committing catastrophic mistakes. A single erroneous price update has triggered automatic liquidations worth millions, without malice and without pause. The lesson is sobering: programmable trust must include safeguards against the world's unpredictability.

And even within code, trust is never static. Software evolves. Vulnerabilities emerge. Governance must adapt. Smart contracts that cannot be upgraded are brittle. Smart contracts that can be upgraded are political. Somewhere in the middle lies the ideal: change that is possible but deliberate, protected by time delays and oversight. The promise of programmable commitments cannot be separated from the duty to verify implementation and maintain vigilance. Audits, formal verification, version control—these are not bureaucratic rituals but the supporting beams of a trust architecture.

What ties these threads together is a recurring motif: truth without tribunal. Distributed systems strive to replace organisational authority with structural guarantees. But guarantees do not eliminate judgement; they relocate it. When we shift trust from institutions to algorithms, we shift responsibility too—to designers who choose parameters, to users who must understand risks, to communities who must coordinate without central leadership.

Consider the consequences. A bank transfer reverses after fraud is proven. A blockchain transfer does not. A legal contract interprets human behaviour; a smart contract enforces strict logic. When a dispute arises, flesh-and-blood judges listen, weigh, deliberate. Code executes. There is dignity in recourse; there is purity in certainty. Which do we want? The answer may differ depending on the situation—or the stakes.

This chapter explores that spectrum. It opens with the fundamentals: why a network must agree before it can act. It reveals how consensus is not a single mechanism but a family of designs making explicit assumptions about adversaries, infrastructure, and incentives. It traces how attackers seek to subvert those assumptions, and how economic design responds in kind. It examines oracle systems that stitch together algorithmic truth and empirical reality. And it ends by considering programmable trust—how we encode intentions into code and how we preserve flexibility without inviting abuse.

Throughout, the focus is not merely how these systems work but *why* their architecture matters for society. Who sets the rules? Who can participate? Who bears the cost when things go wrong? Technologies of trust determine who gets to say "yes", who gets to say "no", and who cannot be ignored.

We live in a world where trust is more necessary than ever, yet harder to place. Our economies run on unseen intermediaries. Our communication depends on opaque networks. Our collective records sit in data centres we do not own and cannot audit. The very fabric of coordination—money, governance, infrastructure—relies on institutions that too often lack accountability or resilience.

So we face a subtle question, one this chapter invites you to confront directly: if we remove the gatekeepers, who or what takes their place? And can we build systems where trust is not a fragile virtue but a resilient property, embedded in the design of the network itself?

Consensus Basics

On 03 January 2009, at 18:15 UTC in Helsinki, the first block of the Bitcoin chain was mined by Satoshi Nakamoto. Embedded in its code was a line from that morning's *Times* headline: *"Chancellor on brink of second bailout for banks."* This was not decoration. It was context. The new system proposed that agreement about value should not depend on governments or banks. Instead, thousands of strangers running software could reach a shared truth about who owned what, without a central referee. It worked. The block remains valid today. Its timestamp is traceable. Its outcome is irreversible. A network had spoken with one voice, despite lacking any single throat to choke.

Consensus is the quiet heart of decentralised systems. If two nodes disagree about the state of a ledger, the system must pick a winner.

If it cannot, there is no system—only fragments. Agreement is not optional; it is oxygen. But the way agreement is reached determines how power flows, how resilient the network becomes, and how costly it is to attack. At the centre of the architecture lies a simple, unforgiving rule: one history, globally visible, must prevail.

Consensus mechanisms are not abstractions. They are rules encoded into behaviour. They determine whether a payment is final in 12 seconds or 60 minutes. They decide whether an attacker needs vast warehouses of specialised chips in Inner Mongolia or simply a large balance in a staking contract. They reveal whether participation is open to anyone who can download software or limited to vetted members. They decide who gets to add new entries to the network's shared memory.

Proof-of-work burst onto the public stage through Bitcoin. It ties influence to computational effort. Each block requires miners to commit energy and hardware. The miner who solves the cryptographic puzzle first earns the right to propose the next block and receives a reward. The visible behaviour is measurable: hash rate, difficulty adjustment, energy consumption. The logic is defensive. To rewrite history, an attacker must control more computational power than the honest majority. That power costs money—hardware purchases, electricity bills—imposed upfront. Cheating is expensive.

Yet proof-of-work's strength is also its vulnerability. The more valuable the network becomes, the more profitable it is to attack—and the more the network must burn in electricity to stay secure. Ethereum, launched in 2015 in Zug and migrated to proof-of-stake in September 2022, made this tension explicit. Its shift away from proof-of-work was framed not as convenience but necessity: the energy costs had become politically and economically untenable.

Proof-of-stake proposes a different commitment. Instead of burning energy, validators lock up capital. Influence scales with the amount staked. If a validator acts maliciously—say, by signing conflicting blocks—the protocol can automatically slash their stake. The behaviour is visible: balances fluctuate, penalties are applied, exclusions are enforced. The cost of attack becomes internal rather than external. An adversary must buy a substantial share of the token supply, which, in theory, aligns their incentives with honest behaviour. But theory meets friction. Wealth concentration can distort participation. If large holders dominate validation, decentralisation becomes cosmetic. Risk shifts from hardware cartels to capital cartels.

Committee-based models, common in permissioned blockchains like Hyperledger Fabric (initial release 2017) or in the scale-optimised Cosmos networks (launched 2019), make a more explicit trade. They restrict validation to a known set of nodes—banks, enterprises, or elected operators. These systems achieve fast finality—often seconds—with low energy overhead. The behaviour feels familiar: performance metrics resemble those of traditional distributed databases. Yet the trust assumption is sharp: a small group must remain honest. If a threshold conspires, the system's guarantees collapse. The lock is strong; the circle of keyholders is small.

Show, name, explain, imply. A transaction sent on Bitcoin might need six confirmations—about 60 minutes—before merchants treat it as irreversible. On Ethereum post-Merge, finality usually arrives in 12–15 minutes. Networks built on Tendermint, such as the Cosmos Hub, often achieve finality within seconds. These delays reflect risk tolerance. A merchant selling coffee values speed. A state pension fund values certainty. Finality time is a metric that reveals political design. It answers the question: how much risk of reversal are we willing to bear?

Consensus is always subjective beneath its mathematics. Participants decide what security model they trust: energy expenditure, capital at stake, bonds among institutions. None is neutral. All encode assumptions about adversaries. Proof-of-work assumes attackers are constrained by physical logistics. Proof-of-stake assumes they fear financial penalties. Committees assume they care about reputation and legal exposure. If those assumptions break, the system frays.

A counter-example demonstrates boundary conditions. In 2021, several smaller proof-of-work chains—Ethereum Classic among them—suffered 51% attacks. Attackers rented hash power from marketplaces such as NiceHash and rewrote history cheaply. The visible behaviour was stark: double-spends, hours of reorganisation, scrambling developers. The security promise had been undermined by commodified computation. Renting replaced building. Proof-of-work's deterrent failed where energy commitment was ephemeral.

Reconciliation lies in acknowledging that consensus design must imagine adversaries with creativity and resources. Threat models cannot rely on perfect rationality. Consider an attacker who seeks censorship rather than theft. They might control enough stake to stall finality, degrade liveness, and undermine confidence without profiting directly. Or picture a state-level actor with subsidies, willing to operate mining farms at a loss for geopolitical leverage. Consensus becomes geopolitical architecture. The economic game expands to include ideology and coercion.

This leads to a crucial behavioural metric: cost to attack. Designers must ask not whether a system works when all behave, but how it behaves when some misbehave. Model the worst actors. Slashing, difficulty adjustment, staking caps—these are visible tools for repricing attack feasibility. If the cost to cheat exceeds the benefit, the network breathes easier. If not, it suffocates.

Consensus also governs access. Proof-of-work opens its doors to anyone with electricity and hardware. Proof-of-stake opens them to anyone with capital—an exclusion by wealth rather than by engineering capability. Committees open them only to trusted institutions. These access models shape who can build economic history. A miner in Lagos can join Bitcoin by plugging in a device. A staker in Boston can join Ethereum by locking up funds. But in a permissioned chain run by European banks, only invited participants can write truth. Participation is political. The question is not merely technical: who deserves authority?

The quiet motif throughout this analysis is the timestamp. Every consensus protocol marks time, not like a clock, but as a sequence of decisions. Each block says: these transactions are before those. Each confirmation says: we are increasingly confident this order will endure. History becomes time anchored in agreement. Attack history, and you attack time itself.

Yet no consensus delivers perfection. Proof-of-work is resilient but costly. Proof-of-stake is efficient but socially brittle. Committees are fast but centralising. Designers must choose the imperfections they can tolerate. Users must understand the risks they inherit. There is no free, apolitical consensus.

We stand now at an inflection. As more assets migrate to decentralised networks, as governance becomes programmable, as real economies depend on these mechanisms, the tolerance for failure shrinks. Consensus that collapses into disagreement threatens livelihoods, not just experiments.

So the forward test emerges, demanding clarity: If consensus builds truth, what scale of trust are we willing to encode in infrastructure—and at what price when assumptions fail?

Incentives and Attacks

On 09 September 2021, the Ethereum network slowed to a crawl. A sudden influx of low-value transactions—thousands per minute—flooded the mempool. The attacker paid just enough gas to keep the queue saturated, but not enough for nodes to dismiss the flood as invalid. Block producers struggled to package meaningful transactions; users saw delays stretch from seconds to minutes; some decentralised applications stalled entirely. No funds were stolen. No protocol rules were violated. The attack worked because it was cheap. It revealed a truth the ecosystem already knew but rarely confronted: a decentralised network behaves according to incentives, not intentions.

To understand where incentives align behaviour and where they fail, we must start with the attacker's perspective. The attacker measures cost. The attacker measures payoff. The attacker measures disruption. A network that assumes benevolence invites exploitation. A network that prices malicious behaviour appropriately forces adversaries to hesitate. In decentralised systems, design is more than engineering; it is economic choreography. A network endures only if honest behaviour is easier, cheaper, and more rewarding than deceit.

The quiet motif here is a scale. A scale weighs intentions against incentives, and it never stays perfectly balanced. Tilt it too far towards permissiveness, and cheap attacks flourish. Tilt it too far towards restriction, and participation collapses. Every protocol lives on this scale.

A central problem in decentralised networks is identity—specifically, the ease of creating many identities at negligible cost. In 2002, Microsoft researcher John Douceur formalised this in a seminal paper presented at IPTPS: the Sybil attack. One actor can masquerade as many, overwhelming systems designed to assume identities map to individuals. Peer-to-peer networks such as early file-sharing systems, and later social networks, learned this the hard way: without identity costs, manipulation becomes trivial. Bitcoin's answer was proof-of-work. Ethereum's answer became proof-of-stake. Other systems rely on stake-weighted voting, admission control, or web-of-trust models. Each method prices identity differently. But none can ignore the Sybil problem without suffering its consequences.

Show, name, explain, imply. A Sybil-resistant protocol forces an attacker to commit something scarce—energy, capital, reputation—before gaining influence. Proof-of-work ties identity cost to joules. Proof-of-stake ties it to locked tokens. Committee-based systems tie it to institutional status. The implications are unmistakable. A well-funded adversary must spend real resources to imitate many identities. A poorly-funded adversary cannot.

But incentives are not stable. They shift as markets evolve, hardware improves, or assumptions decay. When NiceHash, founded in Slovenia in 2014, allowed users to rent hash power, it inadvertently weakened smaller proof-of-work chains. An attacker no longer needed to build infrastructure; they could "borrow" it by the hour. In August 2020, Ethereum Classic suffered multiple 51% attacks using rented hash power. The behaviour was clear: double-spends, chain reorganisations, days of turmoil. Proof-of-work's deterrent—expensive hardware—was circumvented by commodification. The scale tilted.

Bribery introduces a more subtle threat. Validators—whether miners or stakers—face choices at every block. They can include certain transactions, censor others, or reorder them. If a bribe exceeds their expected honest reward, some will defect. This is not conjecture; it is visible in frontrunning markets. In 2021, the rise of MEV (maximal extractable value) on Ethereum demonstrated the potency of incentives to distort block building. Systems such as Flashbots formed to manage the behaviour through auctions. The phenomenon exposes a core dilemma: protocols assume validators act honestly; markets remind us they act profitably. The design must measure incentives with the same precision as cryptographic proofs.

Yet not all attacks aim to profit. Some aim to degrade. Griefing attacks occur when the attacker is willing to pay to reduce the utility of others. Imagine a proof-of-stake network where validators are rewarded for uptime. A malicious actor might accept a personal penalty if it leads to even greater penalties for rivals. The attacker burns £1 to make you burn £10. Rationality breaks because the attacker has different goals. Politics enters the system. Competition becomes asymmetric. The scale tips again.

The mempool flood of September 2021 illustrates another principle: externalities matter. A spammer paid modest transaction fees, but caused widespread delay. Nodes bore the cost of storing, propagating, and evaluating junk. The attack worked because resources were unpriced. Protocol designers responded by adjusting base fees and improving propagation rules. But the lesson remains: anything cheap and unbounded will be exploited. The system must either cap the behaviour or make it costly.

A second named example deepens the pattern. In 2016, the Bitcoin network saw waves of zero-fee transactions originating from clusters in China. The attack clogged mempools and forced miners to prioritise higher-fee transactions. The behaviour revealed a brittleness: fee markets can correct congestion, but at the cost of pricing out low-income participants. Designing incentives is not a purely economic exercise; it carries social consequences. A system that marginalises certain users in the name of security must own that trade-off.

A counter-example demonstrates the limits of pure incentive design. Consider a well-capitalised state adversary. If a government measures value not only in profit but in political leverage, it may willingly lose money to censor transactions or destabilise a rival's chain. The scale shifts because the attacker's goals widen. Cryptographic assumptions hold; incentive assumptions weaken. Protocols designed for rational actors face adversaries who value influence more than revenue. Reconciliation requires acknowledging that no incentive model can fully contain political motive. Threat models must expand.

The motif of the scale appears again in validator behaviour. A validator in a proof-of-stake system measures yield: how much they earn for honest participation. If yields drop, some operators may cut corners: running cheaper hardware, skipping upgrades, or clustering across identical cloud providers. The behaviour looks efficient but increases correlated failure. A single cloud outage can knock out a large fraction of validators. Incentives unintentionally centralise. The system becomes fragile. A decentralised architecture relies on incentives that reward not just participation but diversity.

Every abstraction—security, risk, robustness—must be anchored in behaviour. A fee market demonstrates risk by rising sharply under congestion. A staking contract demonstrates security by slashing those who deviate. A committee demonstrates reliability by consistently reaching rapid finality. These behaviours are measurable—block times, validator uptime, orphaned block rates, slashing incidents. Metrics allow designers to see where incentives succeed or where the scale leans dangerously to one side.

Some protocols experiment with design choices to counter manipulation. Avalanche, launched in 2020 with research ties to Cornell University, uses repeated random sampling among validators to achieve consensus. This makes Sybil attacks more expensive because an adversary must control a large fraction of the sampling pool. Others, like Algorand (founded by Silvio Micali, MIT, 2017), use verifiable random functions to choose block proposers unpredictably. These innovations change the incentives by making influence harder to predict or buy. Yet each introduces new assumptions about randomness, network synchrony, and participant honesty. The scale never balances perfectly.

The question becomes: how do we map attacker costs to system design? The mapping must be explicit. If an attack costs £1 million and yields £500 million, the system invites catastrophe. If an attack costs £10 million and yields political disruption, the system must assume persistent aggression. If an attack costs more than it is worth, the system thrives. Designers quantify this through formal modelling, empirical stress tests, and adversarial simulations. They analyse the cost to isolate nodes, the cost to accumulate enough stake, the cost to spam, the cost to bribe. They calibrate fees, rewards, and penalties accordingly.

But incentives are not static. They evolve with market prices, user behaviour, and innovation. A system secure at £1,000 per coin may be insecure at £50,000 per coin. A system safe when stake is broadly distributed may become brittle as wealth concentrates. A system resistant to hash-power centralisation may weaken once hardware becomes more efficient. The scale's tilt changes over months and years.

The chapter's recurring question—who or what determines truth—narrows here to a sharper point: who or what determines behaviour? A decentralised system survives not because attackers are absent, but because attacking is unprofitable, unrewarding, or too visible to succeed.

So the forward test stands, unresolved but essential: if every system rests on incentives, what happens when a new actor—cheaper, richer, or more determined—steps onto the scale and shifts its weight?

Oracles and Reality

At 14:58 UTC on 14 March 2020, the price feed for ETH on Coinbase briefly showed $0.00. The glitch persisted for less than a minute, but it was enough. A decentralised lending protocol on Ethereum, relying on that exchange's feed through an oracle network, interpreted the sudden collapse as truth. Vaults were liquidated automatically. Borrowers lost collateral they believed was secure. Bots swept discounted assets. Within hours, disputes erupted across forums, GitHub issues, and governance channels. The code had done exactly what it was written to do, without hesitation or doubt. The problem was simple: the world had not actually changed. The oracle had lied.

This event—verifiable, timestamped, and widely analysed—remains one of the clearest demonstrations of the gulf between on-chain logic and off-chain fact. A blockchain can compute with absolute fidelity. It cannot observe. It cannot sample temperature, verify rainfall, detect fraud, or distinguish a transient database error from a real market collapse. Even when thousands of nodes agree on a block, they may be agreeing on something untrue. The tension is structural, not incidental.

This gap gives rise to the motif of the lens. A lens can clarify or distort. A narrow lens captures only a fraction of a scene; a cracked lens warps everything behind it. Oracles are lenses for blockchains. They focus the outside world into a format code can consume, and the quality of that focus determines the truth a system believes.

Show, name, explain, imply. The first claim: blockchains need help seeing. The named example is Chainlink, founded in 2017 and operating across multiple chains. Its network aggregates data from independent providers, signs it, delivers it on-chain, and tracks performance. The explanation: decentralisation reduces reliance on a single source, but it cannot eliminate systemic errors—if many providers read from the same corrupted API, the aggregated value will still be wrong. The implication: diversity of upstream sources matters as much as diversity of oracle nodes.

A second named example sharpens the picture. In June 2022, the lending platform Venus Protocol on Binance Smart Chain suffered a cascade when its oracle misreported the price of LUNA after the token's collapse. Prices streamed from an exchange that had temporarily halted withdrawals but continued publishing stale values. Borrowers used the inflated price to borrow far more than they should have been allowed. Losses were immediate and quantifiable. The behaviour showed a critical fact: even well-designed oracle systems can inherit failures from opaque, centralised venues. The lens captured a broken scene.

The core patterns of oracles fall into several families. Pull-based designs allow smart contracts to ask for data when needed. Push-based designs deliver updates periodically or when certain thresholds are crossed. Some rely on signed messages from central operators; others use decentralised commit–reveal schemes to prevent front-running. Each pattern exhibits distinct failure modes. A push oracle may deliver stale data during outages. A pull oracle may expose request patterns that leak trading intentions. A centralised oracle may be bribed or coerced. A decentralised oracle may be sybil-attacked or collude. The design must acknowledge these behaviours openly.

Metrics validate this. A healthy oracle feed shows tight update intervals, consistent signatures, low variance across providers, and resilience during market volatility. A compromised feed shows lags, anomalies, outliers exceeding statistical norms, or unexplained drops in provider count. These are signals visible to engineers and to attackers alike. Attackers monitor gaps; they measure timing; they exploit misalignment. Oracles are not abstract "sources of truth"—they are concrete systems with observable weaknesses.

To see why oracle design is unforgiving, consider the liquidation logic in lending protocols. A position is safe above a collateralisation ratio: say 150%. If price updates lag by even thirty seconds during high volatility, borrowers may miss the opportunity to top up or close positions. If the feed spikes erroneously, liquidations trigger instantly, because code cannot express doubt. The behaviour is binary: safe or unsafe, solvent or liquidated. This brittleness forces designers to examine the timing assumptions embedded in their protocols. Finality is one matter; reality is another.

A counter-example reveals nuance. MakerDAO, established in 2017, uses a decentralised oracle network but layers it with delay mechanisms and human governance. If a price feed appears incorrect, the system can trigger a circuit breaker, halting certain liquidations. Critics argue this softens decentralisation; supporters argue it prevents catastrophic cascades. The tension is real: absolute automation maximises predictability but increases exposure to untruth; moderated automation introduces subjective judgement but protects against extreme anomalies. Reconciliation lies in admitting that some risks cannot be fully automated away.

Oracles also expose an epistemic problem. Different markets disagree about prices. Illiquid assets swing wildly between venues. Regional exchanges may halt trading due to regulation or technical failure. During the FTX collapse in November 2022, prices for certain tokens diverged sharply across platforms. An oracle must choose which markets to trust, how to weigh them, how to filter noise, and how to respond to fragmentation. Every choice encodes a worldview. This worldview shapes who gains and who loses during shocks. A lens is never perfectly neutral.

The lens motif returns when analysing branch-specific designs such as consensus-embedded oracles. Some blockchains integrate price reporting directly into validator responsibilities. This tightens alignment: validators who misreport can be slashed. But the design also centralises power. A cartel of large validators can coordinate to deliver profitable misinformation, especially during low-liquidity periods. The system gains speed at the cost of surface area; it reduces modularity but increases coupling. Again, the designer must decide how wide or narrow the lens should be.

Recovery strategies matter. After the 2020 ETH zero-price glitch, several teams introduced layered checks: median-of-medians models, deviation caps, time-weighted averages, and fallback mechanisms that halt updates if prices move beyond sane bounds. These features impose friction, but friction can be healthy. A system that pauses to verify prevents irreversible errors. The trade-off is responsiveness. A highly reactive oracle feels faster but is more fragile. A cautious oracle feels slower but may protect against tail risks.

Human involvement, often dismissed in decentralised discourse, remains indispensable. A governance multisig that can freeze an oracle is not an admission of failure; it is an admission of humility. No model can anticipate every market dislocation, software bug, or geopolitical shock. A human override path introduces accountability and context-sensitive judgement. But it must be narrow, auditable, and clearly bounded. A wide override path invites abuse; a nonexistent one invites catastrophe. The lens must be adjustable, not removable.

Another pattern complicates matters further: cross-chain oracles. When assets bridge between blockchains, the source chain's truth must flow into the destination chain. Bridging protocols often rely on external validators or security committees to attest to events. These attestations are a form of oracle input. If compromised, they can trigger synthetic asset inflation, liquidity drains, or wrapped-token depegs. The Ronin Bridge hack of March 2022, affecting Sky Mavis in Vietnam, demonstrated the magnitude of this risk: attackers controlled a majority of validator keys and signed fraudulent withdrawals exceeding $600 million. The behaviour was decisive and quick. The implication is stark: cross-chain messaging is oracle design by another name, with amplified consequences.

A subtle yet crucial failure mode emerges when protocols assume the world will cooperate. Weather oracles for parametric insurance rely on sensors or third-party APIs. Sports oracles rely on score providers. Supply-chain oracles rely on enterprise reporting. Each assumption involves trust, latency, integrity, and potential manipulation. A shipment scanned a few minutes late may flip an insurance payout. A misrecorded rainfall reading may unlock funds. Designing for these realities requires acknowledging that not all facts are deterministic. Some are contested; some are delayed; some are wrong.

At this point, the lens motif clarifies one more dimension: focus requires calibration. Protocol designers must calibrate for volatility, error rates, disputable events, latency bounds, and incentive distortions. They must calibrate for over-reporting and under-reporting. They must calibrate for attackers who spoof sensors or exploit API endpoints. Calibration is both technical and philosophical.

The forward test sits plainly: when truth arrives on-chain, who guarantees that it deserves belief? The system? The market? The oracle network? The humans behind it? The answer shapes every contract that depends on it.

Programmable Trust

On 15 May 2020, the decentralized finance platform Yearn Finance executed a governance upgrade that had been proposed weeks earlier. The process included a time-lock of 48 hours, during which token holders could review, debate, or contest the change before it became effective. When the upgrade finally executed, new parameters for yield distribution went live across multiple vaults simultaneously, without human intervention beyond the prior approval. The system had honoured commitments programmed into code, producing certainty and speed simultaneously. But this demonstration of "trustless" execution also highlighted the fragility inherent in embedding authority into immutable scripts: a single bug, miscalculation, or overlooked edge case could have cascaded losses worth millions.

Smart contracts are programmable commitments: legal-like obligations encoded as executable code. Unlike conventional contracts, they are automatic and non-negotiable once deployed. Their promise lies in their predictability; their peril lies in their inflexibility. A contract that behaves precisely as written may still violate user expectations if assumptions about inputs, timing, or dependencies are incorrect. The quiet motif threading through this discussion is the lock: a construct that enforces commitments without discretion, but which, if misconfigured, cannot distinguish error from compliance.

Understanding programmable trust requires both technical literacy and awareness of system design. Audit and verification become essential tools. Formal methods—mathematical proofs that the code meets specified properties—have been applied in high-stakes contracts, such as the Tezos protocol upgrade in September 2018, where Michel Mauny and colleagues used formal verification to validate consensus-critical changes. The process revealed vulnerabilities that could have led to double-spending or inconsistent ledger states. The implication is profound: trust is no longer solely social; it is computational. Systems depend on humans to reason about adversaries, but enforcement rests on precise execution.

The structure of smart contracts amplifies consequences. Time-locks, like those used in Yearn Finance, illustrate a trade-off between speed and review. A 48-hour delay allows oversight and contestation but also postpones execution for legitimate economic needs. Shorter delays improve responsiveness but increase risk. Each block, each function, each parameter embodies an assumption about participant behaviour, system latency, and market conditions. These assumptions must be explicit, observable, and testable; otherwise, trust becomes brittle.

Upgradability presents another tension. Immutable contracts enforce absolute consistency but cannot adapt to unforeseen requirements or vulnerabilities. Upgradeable proxies—such as those employed by OpenZeppelin frameworks since 2018—allow contract logic to change while retaining state and addresses. The design requires governance, multisignature approval, and careful interface separation. The behaviour is observable: upgrades propagate immediately, state persists, and endpoints remain consistent. Yet the risk is evident: if control over the proxy is mismanaged, a single compromised key can alter logic across millions of dollars of assets. A system built for flexibility introduces a new vector for attacks.

Interfaces are the visible surface where complexity meets participants. Minimising this complexity is crucial for usability and security. A lending protocol, for example, may expose a simple "deposit" and "borrow" button while hiding intricate calculations of interest accrual, liquidation thresholds, and collateral ratios. The abstraction allows participants to act without understanding every line of code, but designers must balance clarity with transparency. Yearn Finance, Aave, and Compound demonstrate different approaches: clear dashboards, on-chain documentation, and layered explanations of risk parameters. These interfaces shape trust as much as the underlying code.

Counter-examples highlight fragility. The Parity multisig wallet exploit in July 2017 demonstrates the consequences of interface complexity coupled with upgradability. A single erroneous library call froze over $150 million in Ether. The code executed exactly as programmed. Governance decisions, intended as safeguards, proved insufficient to prevent disaster. The implication is unambiguous: a contract can be internally correct yet externally catastrophic if design assumptions misalign with human behaviour or emergent interactions.

Audit practices serve as a structural bulwark. Third-party audits, formal verification, fuzz testing, and testnet deployment are all measures to reduce risk. Audit reports for Compound's V2 upgrade in 2020 revealed edge cases in interest accrual that could have been exploited under extreme conditions. Behavioural metrics—transaction throughput, state changes per block, error rates during simulation—allowed engineers to quantify exposure before deploying to mainnet. Audits do not eliminate risk; they make failure probabilistically more visible.

Programmable trust also intersects with social coordination. Governance proposals encoded in smart contracts rely on voting mechanisms. Token-weighted voting can enforce economic incentives, but delegation introduces centralisation. Mechanisms such as timelocks, staged execution, and emergency pause functions create layers of redundancy. When a proposal passes, execution proceeds automatically, but oversight remains possible through structured delays or human intervention. Trust becomes both programmatic and social: code enforces rules, participants shape policy.

The scale motif recurs in finality. Every smart contract decision is a locked state change; it commits to a history that cannot be reversed unilaterally. Time-locks and multi-signature approvals modulate that scale, allowing for review and correction before finality is absolute. Yet every added layer introduces friction and the potential for disagreement or error. Designing programmable trust is therefore a balancing act: maximise reliability and predictability while maintaining flexibility and human oversight.

Another dimension is composability. Contracts interact with other contracts, forming layered systems. A lending protocol may rely on price feeds from oracles, collateral from tokenised assets, and interest calculations from auxiliary modules. Complexity compounds: the behaviour of one contract can propagate to others in ways not fully predictable at deployment. The famous 2020 "bZx flash loan attacks" exemplify this: adversaries exploited interactions between multiple protocols, each individually audited, but collectively vulnerable due to unforeseen cross-dependencies. Programmable trust must account not only for isolated contracts but for the emergent properties of networked systems.

The forward test is clear. Programmable trust offers unprecedented certainty and enforcement. Yet it is brittle if complexity is excessive, assumptions unexamined, or oversight insufficient. Designers must ask: how can we encode commitments that humans rely upon, in systems that anticipate error, abuse, and change? Where should time-locks, multisigs, and interfaces balance control and agility? Every smart contract is both a promise and a potential trap. The design of programmable trust determines whether that promise endures or unravels.

Chapter 4
The Economics of Tokens

In July 2017, Filecoin held its initial coin offering, raising over $250 million in under an hour. The promise was simple yet audacious: to create a network of decentralised storage where participants would earn tokens in exchange for making their disk space available. The token was not simply a speculative asset; it was a coordination tool. By embedding economic incentives into the protocol, the designers sought to align the behaviour of thousands of strangers scattered across the globe, ensuring that storage was reliable, accessible, and continuously maintained. Yet even in this early demonstration, the contours of token economics were apparent: incentives could encourage participation, but misalignment could produce inefficiency, concentration of power, or ephemeral engagement. The world had discovered that money, by itself, was not sufficient; what mattered was the architecture of rewards, the timing of issuance, and the clarity of purpose.

Tokens are often misunderstood as magic money, capable of creating value by virtue of scarcity or hype. In reality, they function as instruments for coordination, embedding rules into economic signals. A token's design shapes behaviour, and behaviour determines whether the system achieves its intended function. Consider storage providers on Filecoin: they stake collateral, deliver proofs of service, and receive tokens only for verifiable uptime. Here, the token encodes a promise—compensation for a reliably rendered service. Its value emerges not from speculation alone but from the utility it confers, the agreements it enforces, and the risks it mitigates. Circular value claims—tokens whose worth depends solely on purchasing themselves—do not coordinate behaviour; they destabilise networks. The distinction between signal and substance is essential for designers, participants, and observers alike.

Utility, governance, work, and reputation form the canonical roles of tokens. Utility tokens grant access or entitle holders to consume protocol resources. Governance tokens allow communities to vote on changes, funding allocations, or protocol parameters. Work tokens reward the performance of verifiable tasks, often tied to resource contribution or task completion. Reputation tokens encode social or technical credibility, functioning as cumulative measures of trustworthiness. The architecture of these roles determines both participation and accountability. A storage provider earns tokens by demonstrating uptime; a validator earns influence by staking tokens; a contributor accumulates reputation by providing sustained quality. Each token type structures interactions, delineates responsibility, and quantifies contribution.

Designing incentives is not a matter of arbitrary issuance. Emissions—the rate at which tokens are created—must balance availability against over-supply. Sinks—mechanisms that remove tokens from circulation—ensure scarcity or counter inflationary pressure. Vesting schedules prevent early actors from exercising outsized influence before networks mature. Participation mechanisms, whether through bonding curves, staking requirements, or contribution verification, align actions with desired outcomes. Bonding curves illustrate the principle clearly: early access to a scarce resource comes at a lower price, but cost increases as demand grows, ensuring that participation signals both interest and commitment. The elegance lies not in complexity but in transparency: participants must see how behaviour generates rewards, and networks must test sustainability beyond mere price appreciation.

Treasuries extend this logic into stewardship. Tokens alone cannot sustain public goods or development infrastructure. Treasuries provide runway and funding mechanisms, allocating resources to client diversity, documentation, research, and critical maintenance. MakerDAO, for instance, distributes grants to encourage ecosystem development, while retaining conservative budget caps and explicit review cadences. Transparency is essential: stakeholders must be able to audit allocations, evaluate conflicts, and observe outcomes. A treasury is a form of programmed generosity, constrained by explicit rules yet responsive to emergent needs. Its governance design directly affects whether incentives remain aligned and whether the network evolves healthily over time.

Measuring real use completes the economic picture. Market price alone is a poor indicator of network health. Real metrics focus on behaviour: active users, transaction volumes, retention rates, and dependency graphs. Unique signers—distinct addresses interacting meaningfully with a protocol—reveal engagement more accurately than speculative wallets. Dashboards visualising participation patterns enable designers to adjust incentives, identify inefficiencies, and correct misalignments before they metastasise. Metrics link tokens to action, reinforcing the principle that economic design is inseparable from observed behaviour.

The motif threading through token economics is alignment. Tokens crystallise coordination, translating intentions into measurable actions. Misaligned incentives produce fragility: participants may hoard, speculate, or free-ride, undermining system objectives. Well-aligned incentives encourage contribution, sustain growth, and distribute responsibility effectively. Filecoin rewarded storage for uptime; MakerDAO allocated treasury funds for ecosystem health; Compound monitored participation to calibrate token distribution. In each case, the token was a lens through which desired behaviour could be observed, measured, and guided.

Circularity, opacity, and excessive complexity are the hazards to avoid. When participants cannot infer how behaviour maps to reward, coordination fails. When token value depends solely on speculative demand, networks become hostage to sentiment rather than function. When incentives are opaque, participants may pursue unintended strategies, concentrating influence or exploiting edge cases. Designers must prioritise clarity over gimmickry, signalling rules, consequences, and entitlements in a manner that participants can understand and trust.

Token economics is thus simultaneously an art and a science. It blends economic theory, cryptography, behavioural observation, and governance design. Each token embeds a microcosm of the system's values: who contributes, who decides, who benefits, and under what conditions. Missteps are visible and often expensive; successes are durable and self-reinforcing. The interplay of issuance, sinks, vesting, treasury management, and behavioural measurement forms a delicate lattice: disrupt one element, and coordination falters; align them effectively, and a network can function with a precision impossible in purely human-managed systems.

The forward tension is unambiguous: if tokens define coordination, how do we design issuance, incentives, and governance to survive scale, volatility, and misaligned behaviour? How do we distinguish between speculative appeal and functional utility? How do we measure the real economy embedded in a network, rather than merely its price signals? These are the questions that frame the exploration ahead, setting the stage for understanding not only how tokens circulate, but how they enable networks to operate, evolve, and endure.

Why Tokens Exist

In August 2017, Filecoin announced its initial coin offering, raising $257 million in under an hour. The offer was not merely financial; it was a promise that participants could earn tokens by providing storage, delivering verifiable uptime across a distributed network of nodes. Those tokens did not derive value from speculative markets alone—they were instruments to coordinate thousands of independent actors, scattered globally, each contributing disk space and bandwidth to a common purpose. The network's viability depended on aligning incentives: a token had to reward service, discourage negligence, and enable growth. The explosion of demand revealed an essential truth: tokens are coordination tools, not magic money. They encode expectations, distribute responsibility, and measure contribution.

Tokens serve as a lingua franca for behaviour. Unlike cash, whose value depends primarily on trust in the issuer or market sentiment, network tokens translate effort and participation into measurable outcomes. They assign rights, obligations, and influence, often simultaneously. Filecoin rewards storage providers for uptime, making the token a tangible metric for network health. Similarly, in the early Ethereum network, miners received ether for validating blocks, reinforcing security while distributing governance influence. The behaviour of participants becomes observable through token flows: who provides capacity, who participates in consensus, who stakes capital. Tokens quantify both service and risk.

The roles tokens perform can be divided into four primary categories: utility, governance, work, and reputation. Utility tokens grant access to protocol services—consuming storage, using a platform, or engaging computation. Governance tokens confer voting rights and decision-making power within a protocol's framework, creating mechanisms for collective control and adaptation. Work tokens reward measurable contributions: storage, computation, verification, or other defined tasks. Reputation tokens encode a history of participation or quality, influencing trust without necessarily moving value directly. These roles are not mutually exclusive; a single token may intertwine utility with governance, or reputation with work. Understanding which role dominates, and under which conditions, is central to effective design.

Consider the example of rewarding storage providers. Filecoin requires nodes to periodically submit proofs of replication, demonstrating that a client's data is actively stored and retrievable. Tokens are disbursed proportionally to performance. The visible behaviour—data availability, proof submission, uptime metrics—aligns economic reward with network utility. The implication is profound: the token functions as both signal and incentive, synchronising disparate actors without central authority. Performance and trust are encoded into the ledger, observable to all participants, and verifiable by protocol rules.

Circular value claims present a persistent hazard. Tokens whose worth depends solely on their own price movement, rather than underlying service or utility, create feedback loops untethered from functional outcomes. Early ICOs, launched in 2017, often promised adoption without requiring demonstrable network contributions. Prices surged and collapsed based on speculation, leaving participants exposed while failing to coordinate productive activity. The behaviour revealed a mismatch between economic signal and actual network function: a token may rise in market value even as its network is dormant or inefficient. Designers must distinguish between tokens that measure participation and tokens that merely measure sentiment.

Utility tokens illustrate this distinction. A token granting access to compute cycles or storage space creates a direct causal link: the more the network is used, the more tokens circulate, and the more participants are rewarded. Governance tokens create indirect links:

holders influence protocol parameters, indirectly affecting value by shaping rules. Work tokens require observable performance. Reputation tokens measure consistency and quality. In each case, the token operationalises expectations into measurable outcomes, allowing the network to self-regulate and participants to understand the consequences of action.

A counter-example demonstrates the limits of this alignment. Social media tokens, in some experimental communities, have attempted to reward engagement without tying value to meaningful contribution. Bots, spam, and coordination failures exploited incentive design. Tokens circulated widely, yet the underlying system gained little resilience or utility. Reconciliation arises in careful engineering: incentives must be measurable, observable, and unambiguous, and the behaviour they reward must be desirable for the protocol's objectives. Tokens without such alignment become speculative instruments rather than coordination tools.

The motif of measurement threads through all token design. Metrics such as uptime proofs, voting participation, transaction frequency, and reputation accrual make abstract intentions concrete. Each token's role defines which metrics matter. Misalignment between metrics and network goals produces inefficiency or vulnerability. Filecoin, Ethereum, and Compound all demonstrate the principle: by embedding performance evaluation into token economics, networks create incentives that guide behaviour in a decentralized environment.

Coordination via tokens also clarifies resource allocation. A system with scarce storage or compute must ration access. Token flows signal scarcity, reward timely provision, and penalise neglect. Bonding mechanisms, staking requirements, or usage-based issuance create feedback loops: participants respond to economic signals, producing outcomes that would otherwise require central management. The network, in effect, becomes self-governing.

The tension in token design lies in the interplay of incentives, scarcity, and trust. A token that perfectly aligns behaviour in one dimension may create unintended consequences in another. Governance tokens concentrated in a small set of holders may centralise influence, undermining coordination goals. Work tokens miscalibrated can over-reward low-quality contributions. Reputation tokens may be gamed through short-term optimisation. Each design decision embodies a trade-off: clarity and effectiveness versus complexity and vulnerability.

Tokens, therefore, exist not to confer value ex nihilo but to operationalise coordination. They transform dispersed, untrusting actors into a network capable of shared action. They encode expectations, enforce rules, and quantify contributions. They bridge the gap between abstract protocol goals and concrete human behaviour. Understanding this foundational purpose—rather than treating tokens as speculative instruments—is essential for any designer, participant, or analyst seeking to build or evaluate a resilient, functional decentralized network.

The unresolved test lies ahead: how can networks design tokens that sustain participation, coordinate complex behaviours, and resist speculation while remaining accessible and comprehensible? How do we ensure that tokens measure productive contribution rather than sentiment? These are the questions that guide every subsequent exploration of token economics, from incentive design to treasury management, from sustainability to measurement of real use.

Designing Incentives

In April 2017, Ethereum's ICO concluded, raising over $18 million to fund development of the network's ecosystem. Early contributors received ether at a fixed rate, but the designers faced a challenge beyond capital accumulation: how to incentivise ongoing participation and contribution as the network scaled. Early participants could speculate, but the system required sustained activity—nodes processing transactions, developers maintaining smart contracts, validators ensuring security. To achieve this, Ethereum's architecture embedded mechanisms for emissions, sinks, vesting, and participation, translating abstract intentions into measurable behaviour. The result was a visible alignment between contribution and reward, producing not just wealth, but coordinated action.

Token emissions determine the supply-side incentives for participants. In Ethereum's early design, block rewards served as emissions, compensating miners for securing the network. The behaviour was observable: miners competed for computational work, validated transactions, and maintained consensus. The amount of ether issued per block was designed to reward participation while limiting inflationary pressures. Without careful calibration, emissions can over-reward early participants, creating inequality, or under-reward ongoing contributors, disincentivising continued engagement. Visible metrics—hash rate, block propagation times, miner participation—allow network architects to measure whether emissions effectively produce the desired coordination.

Sinks complement emissions by removing tokens from circulation, often to manage scarcity and prevent value erosion. Consider transaction fees burned in Ethereum's EIP-1559 upgrade, implemented in August 2021. Fees that would have accrued to miners instead reduced the circulating supply, creating an implicit deflationary effect. The behaviour was clear: participants now experienced both incentive to validate transactions and the perception of scarcity supporting token value. The implication is that sinks are not punitive; they are regulatory instruments, aligning economic forces with network health and long-term sustainability.

Vesting schedules ensure that contributions over time are rewarded proportionally, discouraging short-term speculation. Early Ethereum investors and developers had portions of their allocations locked, releasing gradually. The behaviour encouraged long-term alignment: participants remained committed to maintaining software, securing networks, and building tools. Observable outcomes included reduced sell pressure, sustained development, and retention of human capital critical to network stability. Vesting mitigates the risk of immediate concentration of power and supports predictable participation across multiple cycles.

Participation mechanisms extend incentives into behavioural design. Bonding curves, as implemented in early token sale models like Bancor (2017, Zug, Switzerland), provide a vivid illustration. Tokens are issued at a price determined by a pre-defined curve, where early acquisition is cheaper, but subsequent demand increases cost. The visible behaviour aligns with protocol goals: early adopters are rewarded for commitment, participants signal demand through token acquisition, and resources—be they liquidity, storage, or computation—are allocated efficiently. The implication is that the curve translates abstract demand into actionable economic signals, coordinating participant behaviour without centralised allocation.

Tests for sustainability require moving beyond price metrics. High token prices may indicate demand but reveal nothing about participation, utility, or network resilience. Metrics such as active nodes, transaction throughput, protocol usage, staking engagement, and retention rates reveal whether incentives align with system objectives. For example, a high-volume token market may mask a network with minimal meaningful interaction, whereas a modestly priced token with active validator participation and consistent service provision demonstrates functional sustainability. These behavioural measures expose the difference between speculation and coordination.

Clarity is paramount in designing incentives. Participants must understand how emissions, sinks, vesting, and bonding curves translate into rewards and responsibilities. Complexity, if obscured, produces misaligned behaviour. Early ICOs often used opaque bonus schemes, multi-tiered allocations, and non-linear emission formulas. While mathematically intricate, these mechanisms failed to convey predictable outcomes to participants. Observable behaviour—sudden sell-offs, concentration of holdings, low engagement—revealed the consequences. Simplicity in design supports trust, enables analysis, and reduces unintended gaming of incentive structures.

A counter-example arises in protocols that emphasise novelty over transparency. Certain yield-farming schemes of 2020, like some early iterations on SushiSwap, promised high returns with elaborate liquidity-mining incentives. Participants chased high nominal yields without understanding the mechanics of emissions, sink interactions, or vesting schedules. The behaviour produced short-term spikes but created fragile networks highly sensitive to external price shocks. Reconciling design with real-world behaviour requires grounding incentives in observable, verifiable participation rather than abstract promises.

Treasury and governance interactions further illustrate the importance of incentive clarity. If token distribution or vesting schedules are poorly communicated, participants may misalign behaviour, misinterpret value, or exploit loopholes. Dashboards and reporting tools, as implemented in Compound's governance system (2019, San Francisco), allow participants to observe token flows, voting power, and proposal impacts, translating abstract rules into actionable understanding. The visible link between behaviour and reward stabilises networks by aligning perception with economic reality.

The motif of alignment threads through all incentive structures. Emissions must match effort. Sinks must balance supply. Vesting must preserve commitment. Participation mechanisms must convert signals into meaningful actions. When misalignment occurs, inefficiency and vulnerability emerge; when alignment succeeds, decentralised networks function with emergent coordination equivalent to centralised enforcement but without a single authority. Each token's emission, burn, lockup, and curve is a lever on this alignment scale, requiring careful calibration.

Forward tests emerge naturally: how much inflation is sustainable without diluting long-term engagement? How should vesting schedules balance early risk with persistent contribution? How can bonding curves coordinate access without excluding participants or encouraging speculation? Every decision in incentive design is a trade-off between economic efficiency, social coordination, and protocol resilience. The network's health depends on the accuracy of these calibrations, making incentive design both the science and art of functional token economics.

Treasury and Stewardship

In October 2020, the MakerDAO community approved a proposal to allocate $500,000 from its treasury to support client diversity initiatives across the ecosystem. The funds were earmarked for developers building tools that improved accessibility for underrepresented groups, ensuring that protocol adoption did not concentrate only among early insiders or geographically narrow participants. This decision, visible in on-chain governance records and widely discussed on forums, exemplified the dual purpose of a treasury: it provides runway for critical operations while simultaneously funding public goods that sustain the broader ecosystem. The behaviour of contributors, the allocation of capital, and the visible impact on network health illustrated the importance of careful, principled stewardship.

Treasuries in decentralised networks function as repositories of both security and potential. They underpin operational stability, covering infrastructure maintenance, audits, legal compliance, and incentivising contributions that cannot be captured by immediate token transactions alone. For example, the Compound protocol maintains a treasury that funds ongoing development, bug bounties, and ecosystem grants. Each disbursement is executed according to transparent rules, often governed by token-holder voting, ensuring that participants can observe both process and impact. The implication is that a well-structured treasury mitigates systemic risk by providing predictable resources, supporting network continuity, and aligning incentives with long-term protocol objectives.

Funding public goods requires explicit prioritisation. Grants for developer tools, documentation, or accessibility improvements are investments in the network's collective capacity, rather than assets that generate immediate market returns. MakerDAO's 2020 initiative demonstrates this principle: funding projects that increase client diversity did not produce direct revenue, yet strengthened adoption, resiliency, and equity. Observable metrics—number of active contributors, adoption of tools, user retention—allow the community to measure impact. The implication is that stewardship must balance immediate operational needs with the cultivation of long-term value, recognising that some investments yield indirect but essential returns.

Transparency is central to effective stewardship. Participants must see how funds flow, understand allocation criteria, and evaluate conflicts of interest. Compound, for instance, publishes treasury expenditures, including grants, audits, and operational costs, alongside the voting records of governance token holders. This visibility creates accountability: decisions are both auditable and contestable, reducing opportunities for misalignment or abuse. When transparency is absent, participants may misinterpret incentives, undermining confidence in governance and threatening protocol cohesion. Metrics such as funding cadence, proposal frequency, and approval ratios provide tangible signals of procedural integrity.

Conflicts inevitably arise in any network with shared resources. Treasury stewards may face competing pressures: rewarding developers versus conserving runway, funding experimental tools versus maintaining core infrastructure, or supporting strategic partners versus impartial grants. Explicit mandates clarify boundaries. In MakerDAO, grant programs specify eligibility, purpose, and reporting requirements. These mandates reduce discretionary ambiguity, allowing stewards to act decisively while ensuring that behaviour remains aligned with network objectives. Observable adherence to mandates builds trust, while violations can produce immediate reputational and economic consequences.

Review cadences reinforce stewardship discipline. Regular intervals for treasury audits, proposal reviews, and performance assessments allow networks to respond to emergent conditions without sacrificing predictability. A monthly review of Compound's treasury allocations, for example, provides a structured opportunity to assess expenditure efficiency, measure outcomes, and adjust budgets. The behaviour is procedural: evaluation becomes a routine, observable element of governance rather than an ad hoc reaction. The implication is that disciplined temporal structures enhance reliability and reduce the risk of uncoordinated or impulsive spending.

Conservative budgeting is critical. Treasuries must balance operational runway with strategic investment. Over-allocation can leave protocols exposed to volatility or unexpected shortfalls; under-allocation can impede development, participation, or security. Protocols such as Yearn Finance adopt conservative treasury targets, ensuring that funds cover multiple quarters of development and contingency scenarios. Observing treasury reserves relative to anticipated obligations provides a measurable signal of resilience. Behavioural discipline in spending and cautious projection of future needs reinforce both credibility and sustainability.

Explicit mandates, often codified in governance documents, define permissible uses, allocation thresholds, and evaluation criteria. These mandates are observable commitments, constraining stewards while empowering communities. For example, a mandate specifying that no more than 20% of treasury funds may be used for speculative investments establishes a predictable floor and ceiling for risk-taking. Metrics such as adherence to thresholds, frequency of mandate exceptions, and reporting consistency reveal whether stewards are fulfilling their responsibilities. Clear mandates reduce ambiguity, strengthen trust, and provide participants with actionable insight into decision-making.

Counter-examples illustrate risks when stewardship is underdefined. The bZx protocol, prior to its major exploits in 2020, lacked clear treasury allocation rules for risk management and public goods funding. Funds were concentrated in operational liquidity without structured oversight. When leveraged attacks occurred, the network had insufficient resources to respond effectively, and subsequent interventions were ad hoc. Observable failures—rapid depletion of collateral and loss of user confidence—highlighted the importance of codified mandates, transparent reporting, and structured review cadences. Reconciling the failure with best practices demonstrates that disciplined treasury management is not discretionary: it is essential for network stability.

The motif of continuity threads through effective treasury design. Runway, allocation, and review cycles are not static; they interact with incentives, participation, and emergent risks. Treasuries sustain networks not by fiat or speculation but by disciplined, observable, and auditable management. Every grant, budget decision, or reserve allocation signals priorities, establishes trust, and enables long-term coordination. Networks that neglect these structures risk instability, while those that invest in disciplined stewardship create resilient ecosystems capable of enduring shocks, adapting to growth, and supporting innovation.

Forward tension emerges clearly: how should protocols balance runway against growth, stability against experimentation, and immediate needs against long-term public goods? How can communities design mandates that are explicit yet flexible enough to adapt to changing conditions? Every allocation decision, review cadence, and transparency mechanism embodies these trade-offs, making treasury and stewardship both a technical and social instrument. The answers shape not only where resources flow, but how trust, coordination, and resilience are encoded into the economic fabric of decentralised networks.

Measuring Real Use

In September 2020, the Compound protocol reported over 50,000 unique addresses interacting with its lending and borrowing platform in a single month. At first glance, the figure suggested robust engagement. Yet a closer examination revealed that a substantial portion of activity came from a small subset of high-volume wallets participating in yield farming and liquidity mining schemes. Token circulation was high, but actual user diversity and sustained engagement were far lower. This disparity illuminated a crucial lesson for decentralised networks: price charts and nominal transaction volumes rarely reflect meaningful participation. Observing behaviour—active users, retention, and dependency structures—provides a more accurate lens into network health.

Counting unique signers, rather than speculative wallets, offers a fundamental measure of real engagement. Each signer represents a distinct participant executing transactions, interacting with protocols, or contributing to governance. By contrast, wallets created solely for arbitrage, experimentation, or speculation inflate apparent usage without producing lasting network value. The distinction is observable: signing activity is persistent and verifiable, while speculative accounts often exhibit high volatility and low retention. The implication is that metrics grounded in human or organisational activity are essential for assessing whether incentives, governance, and utility align with intended outcomes.

Dependency graphs extend this analysis by mapping interactions among participants and protocol components. In the Ethereum ecosystem, examining how DeFi contracts interconnect—who borrows, who lends, and which protocols rely on shared collateral—reveals concentrations of risk, influence, and engagement. Observable patterns highlight critical nodes, bottlenecks, and potential cascading failure points. For instance, the bZx flash loan exploit in February 2020 exploited dependencies across multiple protocols, demonstrating that understanding network health requires more than aggregate numbers: the topology of participation matters as much as its volume.

Retention metrics further refine the picture. Measuring how often participants return to transact, stake, or vote over successive periods reveals whether engagement is sustained or ephemeral. In Compound, tracking repeated interactions over three-month intervals showed that while initial adoption was high, only a subset of users continued to participate meaningfully after incentive programmes stabilised. Observable behavioural patterns—transaction frequency, stake persistence, and governance votes—quantify stickiness. Protocols with high retention demonstrate that incentives, user experience, and network utility cohere; those with low retention expose misaligned reward structures or usability gaps.

Dashboards designed to prioritise behaviour over price serve as practical tools for network analysis. Visualising active signers, transaction chains, and dependency graphs allows participants and designers to monitor systemic health in real time. Compound and MakerDAO both publish dashboards highlighting protocol activity, user distribution, and engagement metrics alongside market data. Behaviour-focused metrics allow observers to distinguish between speculative hype and genuine network function, enabling informed adjustments to incentives, treasury allocations, or governance mechanisms. The observable consequence is clearer alignment between network policy and participant behaviour.

A counter-example illustrates the pitfalls of focusing solely on financial metrics. In certain DeFi platforms during 2020 yield-farming booms, token prices soared even as unique user counts plateaued and wallet duplication inflated activity metrics. Participants chasing high returns without interacting meaningfully with the protocol gave an illusion of growth. Behavioural dashboards exposed this misalignment: real participation did not match token velocity. Reconciling these observations demonstrates the necessity of measuring substance rather than surface indicators.

Granular monitoring informs both risk management and incentive design. Identifying critical dependencies allows protocols to mitigate cascading failures, allocate resources effectively, and calibrate rewards. Metrics like median transaction size, network centralisation, and frequency of unique signer interactions reveal where incentives succeed or falter. In Filecoin, observing which storage nodes consistently deliver proofs of replication informs emission schedules and reward distribution, aligning incentives with reliable behaviour. Observable alignment reinforces trust and sustains network resilience.

The motif threading through these measures is alignment between action and reward. Active users, retained participants, and dependency-aware metrics provide feedback loops that inform governance, treasury allocations, and token emission strategies. Misaligned metrics—relying solely on market price or transaction volume—produce incentives that reward speculation rather than service. Networks that prioritise behavioural measurement create more accurate signals for design adjustments, strengthening both decentralisation and resilience.

Forward challenges remain. How should networks balance visibility and privacy when tracking participation? Which thresholds of activity indicate genuine engagement versus gaming? How can dashboards synthesise complex interdependencies into actionable insights for both developers and community participants? Measuring real use demands attention to both quantitative and structural metrics, ensuring that tokens, treasuries, and incentives serve the coordination objectives that define a healthy, functional network.

Chapter 5
Communities as Networks

In November 2019, the MolochDAO in San Francisco approved a grant to fund a new Ethereum infrastructure project. The decision involved a small set of founding members proposing the expenditure, which was then ratified by a wider circle of token holders. The process was not perfect—some proposals languished, some contributors expressed frustration—but it demonstrated a fundamental principle: the DAO was not an end in itself, but a tool to coordinate collective action. Unlike traditional organisations, it formalised mechanisms for participation, delegation, and accountability, translating dispersed individual incentives into coherent group outcomes. The stakes were clear: coordination determined whether resources produced meaningful impact or dissipated in administrative friction.

Communities have always been networks, whether informal guilds, cooperative collectives, or open-source projects. In decentralised ecosystems, this principle is amplified by technology: smart contracts, programmable governance, and immutable records allow participants to act in synchrony without centralised oversight. Yet this coordination comes with limits. Participation ceilings emerge naturally—too many contributors on a single decision can create bottlenecks, fatigue, or burnout. DAOs, therefore, function as instruments to structure activity, define scope, and prevent overreach. A grants DAO differs from a buying club not by philosophy, but by scale, accountability structures, and the granularity of decision-making mechanisms. Each community must calibrate its operational envelope to maintain effectiveness and prevent contributor attrition.

Roles and reputation form the scaffolding of sustained community engagement. Assigning responsibilities, enabling delegations, and codifying non-transferable reputation create predictable patterns of influence. Contributor badges, for instance, may unlock reviewer privileges, providing a visible signal of capability while maintaining reversibility. Observing behaviour over time allows the community to assess competence, reliability, and alignment with shared norms.

Hidden hierarchies—informal power structures that emerge unobserved—pose a risk: they concentrate influence without accountability. Networks that explicitly define roles, permissions, and escalation paths mitigate these dangers, allowing members to act confidently within known boundaries.

Decision-making that scales requires balancing efficiency with inclusivity. Rough consensus, quadratic voting, and council structures provide mechanisms for resolving proposals without collapsing under participation load. Small teams may draft and iterate proposals, while larger groups ratify or veto, creating a multi-tiered process that is both nimble and accountable. Timeboxing and review windows discipline deliberation, ensuring decisions proceed with urgency yet remain thoughtful. Documenting precedents provides memory and continuity: future participants can learn from prior outcomes, reducing repetition, confusion, and internal friction. Observable patterns—how proposals advance, which delegates intervene, how votes are weighted—signal both transparency and systemic maturity.

Conflict and care are inseparable in communal design. Disagreements are inevitable; what distinguishes robust networks is the framework for resolution. Codes of conduct, mediation norms, and structured off-ramps preserve psychological safety and continuity. Forking serves as a last resort, a visible manifestation of unresolvable tension that is costly but sanctioned. Retrospective rituals—regular reflection on decision processes, interpersonal dynamics, and outcomes—embed learning into the network's fabric. Human behaviour, attention, and wellbeing are not incidental; they are infrastructure. Participants must trust both the rules and the environment in which they operate to remain engaged and effective.

The motif threading through this chapter is alignment between structure and action. Networks succeed not because participants are inherently virtuous or intelligent, but because incentives, roles, and processes channel effort toward shared objectives. Whether in a small grants DAO or a sprawling open-source consortium, success is a function of explicit rules, observable outcomes, and predictable pathways for contribution and dispute resolution. Each decision, delegation, and review cycle reinforces or erodes this alignment.

Forward tension emerges in every community: how do networks maintain coordination without centralisation? How should scale, burnout, and scope discipline interact to preserve engagement? How can reputation and delegation remain meaningful while resisting hidden hierarchies? These questions define the frontier of communal design, framing the exploration of roles, decision-making, and care that follows.

From Groups to DAOs

In June 2016, a group of Ethereum developers launched The DAO in San Francisco, raising over $150 million in ether to fund projects across the ecosystem. The initiative collapsed within months due to a vulnerability exploited by an attacker, yet it revealed a critical insight: the DAO was never an end but a tool for coordinated action. Its architecture formalised participation, voting, and fund allocation, translating dispersed intentions into collective outcomes. Unlike traditional organisations, which rely on hierarchical authority, DAOs encode rules, incentives, and workflows directly into protocol, allowing coordination without centralised oversight. The behaviour of participants—proposing, voting, delegating, and executing actions—made the network functionally tangible, even as the initial experiment failed.

DAOs differ fundamentally from informal groups or clubs. A grants DAO, for instance, channels resources toward strategic goals: evaluating proposals, allocating capital, and tracking impact across diverse projects. A buying club, by contrast, coordinates activity to satisfy shared consumption preferences without broader ecosystem effects. Observable behaviours—submission of proposals, approval voting, and follow-through on funded initiatives—define effectiveness. The contrast demonstrates that DAOs are tooling: they structure decision-making and resource allocation to achieve coordination at scale, not a philosophical end. Scope discipline is central; without clearly defined boundaries, contributors risk overextension, engagement fatigue, and diminished impact.

Participation ceilings are natural in any coordinated system. In MolochDAO, San Francisco, 2019, the protocol explicitly limited active voting membership to prevent deliberation bottlenecks and contributor burnout. Metrics such as voting frequency, proposal backlog, and response times indicated thresholds beyond which additional participants reduced overall efficiency. The implication is that DAOs, like any organisation, must balance inclusivity with functional capacity. Contributors facing continuous high-volume demands without role clarity often disengage, undermining the collective purpose.

Defining roles within a DAO mitigates overextension. Delegations and non-transferable permissions allow participants to act with authority in defined domains. Observable behaviour, such as proposal submission rates or review completion, signals effective role execution. For example, contributor badges in certain DAOs unlock reviewer powers contingent on demonstrated participation, creating an auditable hierarchy of competence while maintaining reversibility. These mechanisms prevent hidden hierarchies and ensure that influence emerges from observable merit rather than informal authority.

Burnout remains a subtle risk. The cognitive load of continuous participation—voting, reviewing proposals, and engaging in discussions—can exceed contributors' capacity. Monitoring metrics such as active days, proposal engagement, and discussion participation enables the community to recognise overextension. Protocols may rotate responsibilities, impose limits, or create subcommittees to manage intensity. The behaviour of participants under structured workload constraints reflects the health of the DAO: engaged, productive contributors signal sustainable coordination; overtaxed actors predict attrition and inefficiency.

DAOs also highlight the importance of clear operational scope. Whether managing treasury disbursements, developing protocol infrastructure, or evaluating grant proposals, defining boundaries allows contributors to focus effort without ambiguity. Observable metrics—proposal completion rates, treasury utilisation, and task throughput—provide evidence that scope discipline mitigates misallocation of effort and reduces coordination friction. Conversely, DAOs lacking defined scope risk diffusion of responsibility, redundant effort, and participant disengagement.

A counter-example underscores these risks. The initial DAO experiment of 2016 suffered not only from a security vulnerability but from unclear role definitions and open-ended scope. Contributors could submit proposals without meaningful review structures, and voting mechanisms were overloaded. Observable behaviour—proposal congestion, voting delays, and uneven participation—revealed systemic fragility. Reconciliation lies in careful engineering of participation ceilings, explicit role delegation, and structured workflows, demonstrating that DAOs succeed when designed as tools for action rather than as symbolic ideals.

The motif threading through these observations is alignment between structure and activity. DAOs operationalise coordination by defining who can act, under what circumstances, and how their contributions integrate with collective goals. Participation, delegation, and scope discipline convert dispersed intentions into measurable outcomes. Every proposal submitted, vote cast, and action executed produces observable signals of network efficacy. By focusing on tooling rather than aspiration, DAOs provide a framework for scaling collaborative decision-making while protecting participants from overreach and burnout.

Forward questions persist: how should DAOs calibrate participation ceilings relative to network size and task complexity? What mechanisms best balance inclusivity with efficiency? How can role definitions and delegations remain adaptive without compromising accountability? Addressing these challenges determines whether DAOs function as resilient instruments of coordinated action or fragile experiments vulnerable to overextension and disengagement.

Roles and Reputation

In March 2021, the Gitcoin Grants DAO introduced contributor badges that unlocked reviewer privileges for participants with demonstrated activity in the ecosystem. Within weeks, the system produced measurable changes: contributors who earned badges actively reviewed proposals, validated funding claims, and provided mentorship to new participants. The design operationalised both recognition and authority, linking reputation to specific, verifiable actions. Behaviour became auditable: each badge corresponded to a history of engagement, and privileges could be revoked or reassigned if performance faltered. The outcome illustrated a fundamental principle in decentralised communities: roles and reputation are instruments for coordinated action, not symbolic accolades.

Defining roles within a network allows participants to act predictably and efficiently. In DAOs, this can range from proposal author, reviewer, or validator to treasury steward or protocol maintainer. Observing contributor behaviour—such as proposal throughput, review completion, and voting participation—enables communities to calibrate responsibilities and ensure workload is distributed effectively. The implication is that clearly delineated roles reduce ambiguity, prevent redundancy, and support sustained engagement, while also allowing networks to scale without centralised supervision.

Delegation is a natural extension of roles. Participants unable to engage in every decision can delegate authority to trusted peers, maintaining operational capacity while preserving accountability. In MolochDAO, San Francisco, 2019, delegates executed votes on behalf of members who lacked bandwidth for continuous participation. Behavioural metrics, such as delegated vote frequency and consistency with original intent, provide visibility into whether delegation preserves network alignment or introduces misalignment. Delegation converts latent participation into actionable outcomes, sustaining coordination even as contributor capacity fluctuates.

Non-transferable reputation anchors authority in observable contribution. In Gitcoin, badges unlock capabilities without being sold, transferred, or otherwise monetised. Observable behaviour—frequency of proposal reviews, quality of feedback, and engagement consistency—validates reputation, preventing power accumulation disconnected from effort. Reversibility is critical: privileges can be rescinded if participants fail to meet expectations, ensuring that hierarchy reflects active contribution rather than arbitrary assignment. Networks with opaque or transferable reputational constructs risk hidden hierarchies, where influence becomes concentrated among individuals with symbolic rather than functional authority.

Hidden hierarchies emerge when influence is decoupled from observable action. Early experiments in certain DeFi governance forums, 2020–2021, demonstrated that long-term token holders exerted de facto authority even without active participation. The result was misaligned decision-making: proposals advanced or stalled based on social leverage rather than engagement or expertise. Reconciling this requires explicit role definitions, transparent delegation mechanisms, and auditable activity logs. Observable metrics—review counts, proposal approvals, delegated votes—allow communities to verify that reputation corresponds to contribution rather than latent privilege.

Expectation management reinforces the integrity of roles. Contributors must understand both the scope of their responsibilities and the conditions under which privileges may be revoked. In compound governance experiments, participants were provided with detailed role charters that specified duties, review cadence, and escalation paths. Observable behaviour—proposal compliance, audit completion, and participation in review windows—reflected adherence to expectations. Clear definition prevents role creep, reduces friction, and mitigates burnout, ensuring that participants act within known boundaries while retaining flexibility for reassignment or delegation.

Reputation also functions as a coordination signal. Badges, verified participation, and documented contributions communicate competence and trustworthiness to the wider network. In protocols such as Aragon (Barcelona, 2018), contributor activity is logged and visualised, providing immediate signals of reliability. Metrics such as number of proposals reviewed, treasury transactions validated, or code commits approved reveal actionable patterns of engagement. The implication is that observable reputation enables both informal trust and formal authority, reducing the cognitive load for newcomers and stabilising decision-making across the community.

Burnout remains an ongoing concern. Even well-defined roles and non-transferable reputation cannot compensate for excessive demand. Time-boxed responsibilities, rotation of review duties, and capped delegation limits are observable interventions that mitigate fatigue. Metrics such as consecutive active days, volume of contributions, and response lag signal when participants are overextended. Proactively adjusting workload preserves engagement, maintains quality of output, and sustains reputational integrity over time.

The motif of alignment threads through roles and reputation: authority is meaningful only when it reflects observed contribution. Delegation, badges, and non-transferable privileges ensure that influence emerges from measurable behaviour rather than inheritance or speculation. Networks that maintain visibility, reversibility, and explicit expectations convert dispersed individual effort into coordinated, scalable action. Each interaction—vote cast, proposal reviewed, badge earned—reinforces the fabric of the community, preserving both function and equity.

Forward tension persists: how should networks balance permanence of reputation with the need for adaptability? What thresholds of contribution justify expanded privileges, and how should reversibility mechanisms be applied without undermining trust? Each design choice affects coordination, equity, and resilience, shaping whether communities thrive as networks of aligned action or fracture under hidden hierarchies and unbounded authority.

Decision-making that Scales

In July 2020, the MakerDAO community in San Francisco faced a critical governance decision: whether to implement the Multi-Collateral Dai upgrade, a complex change affecting thousands of active participants and billions in collateral. Small working groups drafted the proposal, scrutinised technical parameters, and modelled financial risks, while the broader community ratified the plan through governance token votes. The process revealed a delicate balance between efficiency and inclusivity: concentrated teams produced coherent proposals, but widespread ratification ensured legitimacy and alignment across the ecosystem. Observable behaviours—proposal submission rates, review comments, and voting participation—demonstrated how distributed decision-making could function at scale when structured with clear roles, time constraints, and layered approvals.

Scaling decision-making requires mechanisms that manage both breadth and depth. Rough consensus allows the majority to signal agreement while accommodating dissent, preventing paralysis in large networks. Quadratic voting, as implemented in Gitcoin Grants, weights votes to reflect intensity of preference, reducing the outsized influence of a few large stakeholders. Councils, committees, or delegated groups provide a bridge between small, nimble teams and the broader membership. The MakerDAO example illustrates this interplay: detailed modelling and risk assessment occurred within specialised teams, while token-weighted ratification engaged the wider participant base. Behavioural metrics—proposal iteration cycles, vote dispersion, and delegate participation—make systemic strengths and weaknesses visible.

Timeboxing and review windows are critical tools for maintaining operational tempo. Decisions that drag indefinitely generate participant fatigue, reduce engagement, and encourage rushed approvals. MakerDAO structured debates into discrete review periods with explicit deadlines for feedback, enabling iterative refinement without compromising responsiveness. Observable indicators such as comment frequency, proposal revisions, and vote timing signal whether the time allocation is effective. Properly calibrated, these windows allow a community to act decisively while ensuring sufficient deliberation, a balance that underpins both legitimacy and efficiency.

Documenting precedents ensures that institutional memory persists. Each vote, proposal, and debate creates a reference point for future decision-making. In Aragon's governance framework (Barcelona, 2018), every action is logged, accessible to contributors, and linked to prior outcomes. Observing historical patterns—how proposals fared, which delegates acted consistently, and which mechanisms mitigated conflict—enables networks to learn, reduce redundancy, and prevent recurrence of preventable errors. The implication is that scaling does not merely require structures for participation but also mechanisms for recording and codifying learning.

A counter-example underscores the risks of unstructured scaling. In certain early DeFi governance forums, 2020, proposals circulated without time-bound review or clear delegation, leading to congestion, low engagement, and inconsistent outcomes. Observable behaviour—stalled votes, repeated amendments, and participant frustration—highlighted systemic inefficiency. Reconciling this requires combining concentrated proposal development, structured ratification, and documented precedent. Only by linking small-scale coordination with large-scale legitimacy can decision-making scale effectively.

Motifs of alignment and visibility recur across mechanisms. Quadratic voting signals intensity of preference, councils distribute responsibility while retaining transparency, and timeboxing establishes predictable rhythms of engagement. Each method relies on observable actions—votes cast, proposals revised, committees convened—ensuring that authority emerges from verifiable contribution rather than informal influence. Networks that adopt these practices translate dispersed individual input into coherent collective outcomes while preserving accountability.

Forward tension remains: how should networks calibrate delegation thresholds against participation size? What degree of complexity in voting schemes preserves fairness without creating cognitive overload? How should documentation balance transparency with digestibility to inform future decisions effectively? Each choice shapes whether communities can scale governance sustainably, maintain engagement, and retain legitimacy as both participation and stakes expand.

Conflict and Care

In November 2016, the Ethereum community faced a defining moment when a vulnerability in The DAO led to the theft of $50 million in ether. The response was not purely technical; it was a crucible for communal norms. Heated debates erupted across forums, chat channels, and developer calls, culminating in the controversial decision to implement a hard fork. Forking was not the default, but a last resort—a structured response to irreconcilable disagreement. Observable behaviours—proposal submissions, debate participation, and voting patterns—revealed both the intensity of conflict and the necessity of clear procedural norms. The

Ethereum case illustrates that the infrastructure of trust is inseparable from mechanisms for managing disagreement.

Conflict in decentralised communities is inevitable. Participants bring diverse priorities, expertise, and incentives. Without formal norms, disputes can metastasise, eroding trust and engagement. Codes of conduct provide a foundation: they articulate behavioural expectations, clarify acceptable channels for dissent, and define consequences for violations. Observable adherence to these codes—comment moderation metrics, enforcement actions, and feedback loops—signals the community's commitment to fairness and continuity. Effective codes translate abstract principles into actionable behaviours, ensuring that conflict is contained without stifling legitimate disagreement.

Off-ramps, or structured exit mechanisms, preserve network health. Forking in Ethereum, Aragon's delegation framework (Barcelona, 2018), and Gitcoin's opt-in exit paths exemplify approaches that allow dissatisfied participants to disengage without compromising remaining operations. Metrics such as withdrawal frequency, delegation reassignment, and proposal abandonment rates reveal the efficacy of these mechanisms. Providing off-ramps reduces escalation, preserves engagement for those remaining, and maintains systemic integrity by preventing conflict from metastasising into paralysis.

Mediation norms operate as the connective tissue between conflict and resolution. In the MakerDAO protocol, San Francisco, 2020, mediation committees reviewed disputes arising from governance proposals, clarified ambiguities, and suggested compromise measures. Observable behaviours—number of disputes resolved without escalation, repeat engagement of mediators, and adherence to recommendations—indicate both the effectiveness and legitimacy of mediation structures. By institutionalising intervention before escalation, communities preserve continuity and allow complex issues to be addressed without undermining participation or trust.

Retrospective rituals complement proactive mediation. Post-mortems of contentious decisions, as implemented in Aragon's 2019 governance review, provide structured reflection: evaluating what decisions worked, which processes failed, and how communication could improve. Metrics such as documented lessons, actionable recommendations, and follow-up adjustments allow learning to accumulate over time. Retrospectives embed organisational memory, ensuring that knowledge is not siloed and that similar conflicts are navigated more effectively in the future.

Psychological safety underpins all of these mechanisms. Participants must feel confident that dissenting views, honest mistakes, and cautious experimentation will not result in personal or professional harm. Observable indicators—active participation rates in discussions, willingness to propose innovative solutions, and low attrition of contributors—signal the health of this safety infrastructure. Networks that neglect psychological safety risk hidden hierarchies, disengagement, and erosion of trust, regardless of technical soundness or governance sophistication.

A counter-example illuminates fragility: the early MakerDAO risk council debates in 2019 initially lacked structured mediation and retrospective processes. Disputes over collateral types and stability fees escalated, leading to public confusion and a slowdown in decision-making. Observable behaviour—proposal delays, repeated clarifications, and uneven participation—highlighted gaps in conflict management. Reconciliation required codifying mediation norms, instituting clear off-ramps, and embedding retrospective reviews into the governance rhythm.

The motif threading through these practices is resilience through structure. Conflict is neither abnormal nor necessarily destructive; it becomes an asset when channels for expression, resolution, and reflection are clearly defined. Codes of conduct, off-ramps, mediation, and retrospectives transform abstract disagreement into observable, actionable outcomes. Each mechanism creates feedback loops that preserve both trust and operational continuity.

Forward tension remains: how should communities calibrate the intensity and frequency of mediation versus participant autonomy? When does escalation justify structural intervention such as a fork? How can psychological safety be measured and preserved as networks scale? Each decision shapes whether conflict acts as a generative force for learning or a destabilising force that fragments coordination.

Chapter 6
Privacy by Design

In 2019, a journalist in Hong Kong faced targeted harassment while coordinating civic reporting under heavy surveillance. Every message, contact, and digital action carried risk; even innocuous communications could expose collaborators. The tools available were rudimentary: encrypted messaging, pseudonymous accounts, and cautious operational security. Yet these measures only partially mitigated exposure, illustrating that privacy is not merely a feature—it is a foundational necessity. Observable behaviours, such as cautious account creation, compartmentalised communication channels, and selective sharing, demonstrate how humans navigate risk when the system itself does not enforce protection by default. The paradox is stark: a network designed for openness can simultaneously render participants dangerously visible.

Privacy by design begins with threat modelling for humans. Users encounter concrete risks—harassment, doxxing, and systemic surveillance—that vary with context, adversary capabilities, and platform architecture. Mapping these threats requires attention to both technical and social vectors. Activists, journalists, and everyday participants alike navigate overlapping adversarial pressures, from malicious actors exploiting weak protocols to automated scraping by commercial platforms. Behavioural observation, such as patterns of account rotation, multi-layered authentication, or segregated digital identities, provides insight into how risk manifests in practice and where system defaults fail novice users. Prioritising protective defaults mitigates inadvertent exposure, ensuring that privacy is embedded rather than optional.

Selective disclosure represents a critical design strategy. Zero-knowledge proofs, cryptographic attestations, and minimal disclosure mechanisms allow users to verify attributes without revealing unnecessary information. For instance, proving age without sharing a full birthdate reduces friction while preserving confidentiality. User behaviour—choosing whether to reveal credentials, managing consent prompts, and interacting with layered interfaces—illustrates the trade-offs between privacy and usability.

The computational overhead of zero-knowledge protocols and the cognitive load of consent management require careful design; systems must respect human limitations while maintaining rigorous guarantees. Observing interaction patterns illuminates how privacy can be operationalised without diminishing participation.

Public ledgers complicate privacy further. Transparency enables accountability, yet indiscriminate exposure of transaction histories, ownership, and participation can endanger individuals. Technical strategies such as coin mixing, shielded pools, and account abstraction patterns allow for role separation and selective visibility. In projects like Zcash (2016, MIT Media Lab), shielded transactions demonstrated that privacy-preserving ledgers could coexist with regulatory transparency. Observable indicators—patterns of shielded transaction adoption, use of pseudonymous identities, and role-specific account segmentation—reveal both the efficacy and the limits of privacy mechanisms. Reconciling openness with confidentiality requires explicit design decisions, cultural norms, and lawful frameworks.

Compliance can itself be framed as an interface challenge. Rather than embedding surveillance into every interaction, systems can encode rules in machine-readable policies and attestations, enabling applications to filter sanctioned actors without monitoring the entire user base. Observable behaviours—how apps enforce constraints, users respond to automated checks, and systems handle exceptions—show the effectiveness of privacy-aware compliance. Platforms that integrate regulatory constraints as design features, rather than afterthoughts, balance principle and pragmatism. Participants gain predictability without sacrificing confidentiality, and network operators maintain legitimacy without eroding trust.

A recurrent motif emerges: visibility is a resource that must be intentionally allocated. Each design choice—default privacy settings, selective disclosure protocols, ledger transparency, and compliance interfaces—affects who can see what, when, and under what conditions. Observing patterns of disclosure, interaction, and adherence to protective defaults illuminates the consequences of these choices. Privacy is not binary; it is a spectrum shaped by technical affordances, user behaviour, and adversarial capacity.

Forward tension remains: how should systems balance transparency with individual protection? When do protective defaults hinder legitimate participation, and when does excessive openness jeopardise safety? How can privacy guarantees scale across diverse users with varying technical literacy and risk exposure? Each decision defines the contours of trust, safety, and agency in digital networks, and sets the stage for practical strategies that embed privacy as a core principle rather than an optional add-on.

Threat Modelling for Humans

In 2014, the Hong Kong pro-democracy activist Joshua Wong navigated a digital environment fraught with surveillance and targeted harassment. Every message sent, every organisational plan shared online carried measurable risk. Mobile devices and social networks were simultaneously tools and vulnerabilities; observable behaviour—rotating accounts, encrypted messaging, and compartmentalised communication—demonstrated how humans adapt to high-threat contexts when technology is permissive but not protective. This case illustrates that threat modelling must begin from the human perspective, not the system's architecture alone.

Threat modelling for humans starts by mapping concrete risks. Harassment, doxxing, and state or corporate surveillance are immediate, measurable threats with varying likelihood and impact depending on context. In 2018, the Myanmar journalists targeted by automated scraping tools revealed that even ostensibly benign platform features could be weaponised. Metrics such as frequency of contact tracing, unsolicited exposure of identifiers, and cross-platform account linkages highlight how adversaries exploit systemic weaknesses. By observing real-world behaviours—such as adoption of pseudonyms, selective information disclosure, and staged interactions—designers can prioritise interventions that protect the most vulnerable participants without imposing undue cognitive overhead.

Identifying adversaries and their capabilities is essential. They range from individual harassers to coordinated state actors, each with varying technical sophistication and motivation. For instance, in the 2019 Hong Kong protests, both local and international surveillance actors leveraged network analysis to identify protest organisers. Observable effects included selective arrests, account compromises, and sudden drops in participation. Mapping these adversaries reveals the spectrum of threats: automated scraping, social engineering, and coordinated disinformation campaigns. Designers must calibrate protections to threat capabilities, aligning system affordances with realistic scenarios rather than idealised assumptions.

Defaults play a critical role in protecting novices. Users unfamiliar with cryptography, privacy-preserving tools, or multi-account management are particularly exposed. Platforms that require manual configuration for security—such as optional two-factor authentication or default public profiles—shift the burden onto individuals, often leading to inadvertent exposure. Observing novice behaviour, such as repeated password resets, accidental public sharing, or unverified contact acceptance, indicates areas where protective defaults can reduce risk without limiting participation. Implementing safe-by-default settings—encrypted messaging, automatic pseudonym generation, and default privacy tiers—mitigates the cognitive load on new users while preserving operational flexibility.

Case studies illuminate the balance between usability and threat mitigation. Signal's deployment in Myanmar (2017–2018) demonstrated that end-to-end encryption alone was insufficient; user education, safe-contact verification, and metadata minimisation were equally crucial. Observable metrics—installation rates, retention of verified contacts, and error frequencies in message handling—provided insight into system effectiveness. Conversely, platforms that emphasise openness without clear protective defaults, such as early Facebook groups used for activist coordination, exposed users to targeted harassment and doxxing. Analysing these examples shows that technical capability without human-centric design leaves participants vulnerable, while over-engineered barriers risk alienating users.

Threat modelling must account for adversary evolution. Automated scraping, deepfake identification, and cross-platform correlation increasingly exploit seemingly trivial disclosures. For instance, linking a pseudonymous account to a real-world identity via image metadata or posting patterns is a predictable but persistent vector. Observing these behaviours and incidents allows designers to anticipate future risks, adapting system defaults and protocols accordingly. Metrics such as incident frequency, breach scale, and recovery time offer measurable indicators of resilience and inform iterative design improvements.

A recurrent motif emerges: human behaviour is both the locus of vulnerability and the vector for resilience. Every interaction, disclosure, and fallback reveals latent risks and adaptive strategies. By centring threat models on observable human decisions, designers prioritise protective measures that are practical, context-sensitive, and minimally intrusive. Mapping adversaries, understanding capabilities, and embedding default safeguards collectively shift the burden from individuals to system design, fostering safer participation without impeding agency.

Forward tension remains: how should systems calibrate protective defaults for diverse user populations? When does usability override maximal security, and when is intervention mandatory? How can threat models remain current as adversaries evolve and human behaviour adapts? These questions define the design space for privacy-aware systems, ensuring that human-centric threat modelling is both actionable and enduring.

Selective Disclosure

In 2019, the city of Austin, Texas, piloted a digital identity programme allowing residents to prove their age for access to adult-oriented services without revealing birthdates or full government identifiers. The initiative relied on cryptographic techniques that ensured minimal disclosure of personal data while maintaining verifiable authenticity. Users could demonstrate eligibility in seconds, avoiding repeated identity checks and the risks of leaking extraneous information. This case underscores a fundamental shift in digital interactions: the ability to reveal just enough information to satisfy a verifier, without overexposing oneself.

Selective disclosure is anchored in the concept of zero-knowledge proofs (ZKPs), a class of cryptographic methods in which one party proves a statement is true without revealing any additional information. For instance, proving one is over eighteen to access a service does not require exposing a birthdate, place of birth, or legal identifiers. ZKPs operationalise privacy by design: they create mathematically enforceable boundaries between necessary and extraneous data. The practical implications extend to financial services, healthcare, and social networking, where the cost of over-disclosure can be reputational, legal, or even physical. In 2020, the European Blockchain Services Infrastructure explored ZKPs to enable cross-border identity verification while respecting GDPR's data minimisation principles.

Implementing selective disclosure introduces both technical and human considerations. On the technical side, computation and communication overhead are non-trivial. Generating proofs often requires hundreds of milliseconds for small statements and several seconds for more complex claims. Systems such as zk-SNARKs or zk-STARKs, while highly efficient compared with earlier ZKP constructions, still impose resource constraints, particularly on mobile devices or low-bandwidth environments. Designers must balance proof complexity with user experience, ensuring that cryptographic robustness does not create friction that drives users toward insecure workarounds.

Equally important is the cognitive load on users. Presenting choices for disclosure—what to share, with whom, and under what conditions—can overwhelm even technically literate participants. UX patterns such as staged consent, contextual prompts, and progressive disclosure mitigate this risk. Mozilla's Persona system (2011–2016) experimented with selective authentication, allowing users to present a verified email without revealing additional details. While the system ultimately failed due to adoption barriers, it demonstrated how interface design shapes privacy outcomes: users must clearly understand what is disclosed, why, and how to revoke or limit access.

Selective disclosure also intersects with regulatory compliance and auditing. Consider financial platforms performing know-your-customer (KYC) checks. Traditional processes demand extensive document sharing, increasing exposure to data breaches. By contrast, a ZKP-based system allows a user to prove regulatory compliance—such as residing in a particular jurisdiction or maintaining minimum account balances—without revealing account history or identifying details. The implication is profound: regulators can verify compliance without centralising sensitive data, reducing systemic risk. The World Bank's 2021 pilot of blockchain-enabled identity attestations in the Pacific Islands exemplifies this principle, providing verifiable benefits while safeguarding privacy.

Applications extend to social interactions. Platforms increasingly require attestations for trust signals—age, reputation, membership status—without exposing broader personal histories. For example, gaming communities have begun experimenting with reputation badges that validate achievements without linking them to identifiable profiles. This approach reduces harassment risk, preserves anonymity, and strengthens trust networks. Conversely, early implementations of identity-linked forums without selective disclosure often resulted in doxxing incidents or harassment, illustrating the consequences of full disclosure in complex social systems.

Designers must anticipate adversarial attempts to circumvent minimal disclosure. Correlation attacks, metadata analysis, and side-channel information can compromise privacy even when cryptographic proofs are robust. Systems must therefore embed layered protections: ephemeral credentials, randomized proof timing, and decoupling of identifiers across contexts. Observing real-world deployments, such as zkRollup-based payment networks in 2022, highlights the tension between verifiable utility and exposure: users benefit from provable balances without revealing transaction histories, yet sophisticated linkage techniques can partially re-identify participants if protocols are misconfigured.

A recurring motif in selective disclosure is the trade-off between utility and exposure. Every proof, badge, or credential carries potential value and potential risk. Mapping these trade-offs requires careful analysis of use cases, adversary capabilities, and human behaviour. Designers must measure both adoption rates and inadvertent leakage, iterating interfaces and protocols to align usability with security. Moreover, layered consent mechanisms, cryptographically enforced minimal sharing, and revocation paths collectively create a resilient system capable of adapting to evolving threats.

Forward tension persists: how can systems scale selective disclosure while maintaining intuitiveness? What metrics capture real-world success—adoption, retention, or actual minimisation of sensitive data exposure? How can interfaces convey complex cryptographic assurances without overwhelming users? Navigating these questions defines the next frontier in privacy-preserving design, where selective disclosure transforms the architecture of trust itself.

Public ledgers, private lives

In March 2021, the decentralized finance platform Tornado Cash became a focal point in the debate over blockchain transparency and user privacy. By allowing Ethereum transactions to be obfuscated through a network of smart contracts, Tornado Cash enabled participants to conceal the source and destination of funds while preserving verifiable settlement on a public ledger. The paradox was striking: the blockchain itself recorded every transaction, yet the identities behind those transactions remained shielded. This duality illustrates the essential challenge of designing digital systems that are simultaneously transparent, accountable, and protective of individual privacy.

Public ledgers are inherently auditable. Bitcoin's genesis block, mined by Satoshi Nakamoto in January 2009, exemplifies an immutable record where every coin and transaction is traceable. This transparency creates trust, enables auditing, and deters manipulation. However, the very same visibility exposes sensitive patterns. For a civic activist or journalist, associating addresses with real-world identities can create personal risk. The tension between ledger integrity and personal confidentiality is not theoretical; it shapes the design of every blockchain and distributed system.

Reconciling these needs requires a combination of cryptographic techniques, interface design, and operational discipline. Mixing services, shielded pools, and account abstraction offer practical strategies for separating transactional metadata from personal identifiers. In the case of Zcash, implemented in 2016 by the Electric Coin Company, shielded addresses allow users to transact privately while auditors can still verify network integrity through selective disclosure of zero-knowledge proofs. Similarly, Ethereum's account abstraction proposals permit the decoupling of signing keys, account roles, and execution logic, enabling one identity to assume multiple pseudonymous roles for governance, payment, or reputation purposes.

Mixing services provide one of the earliest approaches to obfuscation. By aggregating multiple inputs and outputs in a single transaction, these services obscure linkages that could reveal ownership patterns. Tornado Cash employs zero-knowledge proofs to ensure that funds withdrawn from the pool cannot be associated with deposits, but the technique imposes operational complexity: users must manage cryptographic notes securely, and the system's design must prevent replay attacks. Despite these safeguards, the method is not foolproof. Regulatory interventions and on-chain forensic techniques can partially deanonymise participants, revealing the limits of purely technical privacy solutions.

Shielded pools extend this concept by enabling selective visibility. In Zcash, shielded transactions can be audited without exposing individual participants, striking a balance between transparency and confidentiality. This architecture also allows regulatory and governance bodies to verify protocol integrity or compliance obligations without full access to personal data. The implications are substantial: privacy can coexist with accountability if cryptographic proofs are coupled with thoughtfully constructed institutional roles. By comparison, earlier Bitcoin-based mixers such as ChipMixer (active 2017–2021) lacked robust cryptographic guarantees, leaving users exposed to deanonymisation via transaction clustering and timing analysis.

Account abstraction introduces a complementary layer. By separating authentication from transaction execution, a single user may operate multiple pseudonymous accounts for different purposes: one for voting in a DAO, another for personal payments, and a third for client interactions. This separation reduces the risk of correlation attacks while enabling role-based accountability. For example, a decentralized grants DAO might issue distinct addresses for proposal submission, voting, and fund disbursement. Each address maintains auditability within the network but protects the identity and context of its operator, demonstrating that ledger visibility and privacy can be functionally orthogonal.

Interfaces are critical in managing the interplay between public ledgers and private data. Users must understand which transactions are exposed, which remain confidential, and how permissions propagate across roles. UX patterns such as staged consent, clear risk indicators, and ephemeral credentials help prevent inadvertent exposure. In practice, systems that fail to communicate these nuances—whether due to opaque dashboards or inconsistent documentation—generate behavioural risk: users may bypass privacy features, reuse addresses across contexts, or misinterpret the scope of their disclosures. These failures illustrate that technical guarantees alone are insufficient; interface design, education, and cultural norms are integral to effective privacy enforcement.

Lawful use and community norms form a second axis of reconciliation. While shielded transactions or pseudonymous roles preserve privacy, actors remain bound by legal frameworks and network rules. Protocols can embed compliance checks that respect privacy: smart contracts may enforce sanctions or policy constraints without requiring surveillance of unrelated participants. In 2022, the European Blockchain Services Infrastructure explored machine-readable attestations that allowed nodes to filter transactions from sanctioned addresses while maintaining overall transactional confidentiality. The insight is that privacy and compliance need not conflict; they require careful alignment of cryptography, incentives, and operational policy.

Ultimately, the motif threading public ledgers and private lives is duality: transparency versus confidentiality, visibility versus control, accountability versus anonymity. Every design decision navigates this tension, from mixer construction to account abstraction, from interface design to regulatory alignment. Cryptography provides the tools, but human factors and governance define their efficacy. Designers must anticipate adversarial analysis, user error, and evolving legal constraints, embedding resilience into both technology and culture.

The unresolved question persists: how can digital networks scale transparency for societal trust while preserving individual confidentiality in heterogeneous environments? How should interfaces communicate the boundaries of privacy without overwhelming users? How can norms and enforcement coexist with pseudonymity? Addressing these challenges defines the future of blockchains and distributed systems, where public ledgers serve society, and private lives remain respected.

Compliance as interface

In September 2022, Circle, the issuer of the USDC stablecoin, updated its infrastructure to integrate automated filtering of sanctioned wallets while maintaining privacy for the broader user base. The modification did not surveil every transaction or expose unrelated accounts; instead, it relied on machine-readable attestations of compliance. This approach reframed compliance from a burdensome, opaque regulatory requirement into an interface problem: how can a system mediate rules, guide user behaviour, and enforce law without undermining privacy or usability? The Circle example illustrates a broader design principle that extends far beyond stablecoins: compliance, when treated as an interface, can be anticipatory, scalable, and minimally invasive.

Traditional compliance systems often operate as afterthoughts, layered atop platforms with minimal integration. In contrast, interface-centric compliance embeds policy interpretation into the user experience. By transforming rules into computational artefacts—machine-readable policies, attestations, and executable constraints—applications can actively guide actions without exposing unnecessary data. For instance, a wallet application may block a transaction from a sanctioned address without querying the broader network, ensuring both legal adherence and user privacy.

This reduces risk while maintaining operational efficiency, and avoids the trap of omniscient monitoring that erodes trust.

The motivation for reframing compliance in this way stems from the dual imperatives of digital governance: enforceable standards and human-centred usability. Users, particularly novices, should not bear the cognitive load of parsing complex regulations; nor should developers shoulder the burden of manual audits for routine transactions. By providing clear, consistent interfaces that encode obligations directly into workflows, systems can both scale and adapt. Ethereum-based protocols such as OpenZeppelin's Governance modules exemplify this: rules for quorum, voting thresholds, and time-locked operations are embedded in smart contracts, enabling participants to understand and predict outcomes without external legal consultation.

Machine-readable policies are central to this design paradigm. By encoding sanctions, eligibility criteria, or access rules in structured formats, applications can automatically enforce constraints while retaining the flexibility to evolve. For example, the Interledger protocol standardises account-level conditions that can be read and interpreted by disparate systems, allowing compliance logic to travel with the transaction rather than being hard-coded into each platform. This modularity enables rapid adaptation to regulatory changes and supports cross-platform interoperability without centralising sensitive data.

Attestations provide another crucial layer. A financial application may request a verifiable attestation confirming that a wallet or user satisfies a particular compliance criterion, such as residency or age, without exposing additional identifiers. Civic, a UK-based identity platform piloted in 2019, demonstrated the practical value of selective attestations: users could prove their eligibility for services without transmitting full identity documents. In blockchain contexts, zero-knowledge proofs extend this principle, allowing systems to verify conditions on-chain without revealing extraneous data. The implication is profound: trust in compliance can be derived from cryptographic assurance rather than pervasive monitoring.

Interface design also mediates the tension between principles and pragmatism. Policies may be complex, nuanced, and jurisdiction-dependent, yet interfaces must present them clearly and unambiguously. Time-bound review windows, staged consent flows, and contextual warnings reduce cognitive load and prevent inadvertent non-compliance. Consider a decentralized exchange implementing sanctions checks: rather than halting all transactions, it may display an alert, request confirmation, and validate against up-to-date machine-readable lists. Users retain agency, the platform retains compliance, and the system respects the limits of both technical and human capacity.

Failures in interface-centric compliance illustrate the stakes. In 2021, several DeFi platforms suffered from delayed or incomplete sanctions updates, resulting in frozen assets or inadvertent interactions with prohibited addresses. The problem was not technical infeasibility but interface opacity: the policy existed, but neither users nor automated systems could easily interpret or act on it. By contrast, platforms that visualise compliance states—flagging restricted accounts, indicating attestations, and providing clear remediation paths—reduce errors, litigation risk, and community distrust.

The motif threading these examples is mediation: compliance as a bridge between law, technology, and human behaviour. Interfaces translate abstract rules into actionable, observable outcomes. Machine-readable policies encode legality, attestations provide verifiable assurances, and user-facing workflows communicate obligations effectively. Together, these elements create a network of trust that does not rely on surveillance or brute-force enforcement.

Challenges remain. Policies must be updated in real time, attestations must remain trustworthy, and interface complexity must not overwhelm users. Conflicts between jurisdictions, evolving definitions of illicit activity, and adversarial behaviour test the resilience of these designs. Nonetheless, treating compliance as an interface provides a framework to navigate these tensions systematically, enabling digital systems to scale, respect privacy, and maintain lawful operation.

The open question persists: how can platforms standardise machine-readable compliance while accommodating diverse legal regimes? How can interfaces convey obligations without inundating users? Balancing adaptability, clarity, and trust will define the next generation of systems where compliance is not a hidden backend process but a transparent, usable layer embedded in the user experience.

Chapter 7
Storage Without Servers

In June 2018, the city of Medellín, Colombia, faced a sudden spike in civic data requests following a local election audit. The municipal archives, held in a conventional server cluster, strained under repeated queries, with certain files duplicated across multiple locations to meet demand. Yet a parallel experiment was quietly unfolding: researchers deployed a peer-to-peer, content-addressed storage system, retrieving critical documents by their content ID rather than server path. Even as servers faltered under load, files retrieved through their hashes remained intact and verifiable, demonstrating a principle that would reshape assumptions about digital storage: integrity need not depend on centralised machines.

This chapter examines the architecture and philosophy behind storage without servers. Content addressing—using hashes as identifiers—provides immutability and enables deduplication across a network of nodes. Unlike traditional systems, where identical files occupy separate storage and version control is often manual, decentralised storage ensures that identical content converges on a single canonical representation. This not only reduces wasted space but also simplifies versioning and retrieval, allowing a peer to fetch a file from any node holding it, provided the content ID is known. Pinning responsibilities, while imposing obligations on certain participants, further guarantee that critical data persists over time.

Availability and incentives are the engine behind resilient, serverless storage. Networks such as Filecoin and Arweave demonstrate economic coordination at scale: storage providers earn rewards for proving continued custody of data, often using proofs of space-time, while clients gain assurance of reliability. These mechanisms are not abstract; they define service-level expectations and costs, enabling comparisons with traditional cloud pricing. Honest reporting, transparency in replication, and clearly defined service-level objectives (SLOs) become critical, aligning incentives with practical needs rather than speculative promises.

Beyond integrity and persistence, the lifecycle of data demands careful orchestration. Hot, warm, and cold storage tiers adapt to access patterns, from frequently updated civic datasets to long-term archival material. Garbage collection, pruning of obsolete entries, and recovery strategies must be disciplined and predictable. Metadata practices, often overlooked in decentralised contexts, underpin these processes, allowing systems to track provenance, lineage, and recoverability without central authority. In this way, decentralised storage marries the reliability of traditional archives with the flexibility and fault tolerance of distributed networks.

Edge and offline-first design principles further extend the resilience of serverless storage. Local-first applications—such as peer-synchronised note apps—illustrate how users can maintain continuity of access even amid intermittent connectivity. Conflict resolution and CRDT-based replication ensure that concurrent edits reconcile gracefully, delivering a seamless user experience while preserving data integrity. These principles emphasise that storage systems are not merely repositories but infrastructures for human workflows, designed to absorb both technical and behavioural variability.

The motif threading these considerations is autonomy: enabling individuals and organisations to store, retrieve, and verify content without reliance on central servers. Content addressing anchors integrity, incentives drive availability, lifecycles manage temporal relevance, and edge-first approaches safeguard continuity. Each element interacts with the others, creating a resilient ecosystem where storage is decoupled from centralised machines, yet remains dependable, accountable, and usable.

Yet challenges remain. Economic incentives must remain sustainable without introducing prohibitive costs. Pinning strategies require coordination to prevent accidental data loss. Metadata discipline and recovery protocols must scale across heterogeneous networks. Balancing these considerations demands design foresight, careful monitoring, and iterative improvement. The questions that follow—how to structure incentives, define SLOs, manage lifecycles, and handle offline-first reconciliation—are not merely technical; they are architectural imperatives that shape the future of decentralised storage.

Storage without servers is more than a technical choice; it is a philosophy of resilience, autonomy, and integrity. By framing storage as a networked, incentivised, and locally resilient system, this chapter sets the stage for understanding how data can persist and remain trustworthy in environments where centralisation is neither desired nor necessary. It is a framework for thinking beyond the server rack, towards a world where information is anchored in protocols, economics, and human-centred design.

Content addressing

In November 2017, the OpenBazaar project demonstrated a remarkable retrieval: a digital artwork stored by one participant in Boston was requested and correctly fetched by a peer in Amsterdam using only a content identifier. No server mediated the transaction; the network relied entirely on hashes to locate the file. The result was immediate verification: the retrieved file's hash matched the original, ensuring authenticity and integrity across a distributed system. This example underscores the principle at the heart of content addressing: the identifier is not a location, but a fingerprint of the content itself.

Content addressing replaces traditional file paths with content IDs, typically cryptographic hashes, which uniquely represent the file's data. Unlike hierarchical filenames or server locations, a content ID (CID) inherently verifies integrity: any alteration in the file immediately changes the hash, alerting recipients to tampering or corruption. This property is foundational for distributed storage networks, where files are replicated across heterogeneous peers with varying reliability. By decoupling identity from location, CIDs allow retrieval from any node that possesses the content, simplifying redundancy, and reducing dependency on centralised infrastructure.

Deduplication is a natural consequence. If multiple participants store identical files, a single CID references all copies, preventing redundant storage and lowering network overhead. For instance, in

IPFS, uploading the same dataset twice generates the same CID, allowing peers to retrieve existing copies rather than storing duplicates. Versioning is similarly streamlined: content changes produce new hashes, creating an immutable history of modifications. Systems like Git illustrate this principle; each commit hash acts as a content ID, enabling precise reconstruction of past states. In large-scale distributed storage, this approach eliminates ambiguity in data provenance and supports reproducible workflows.

Pinning responsibilities form another critical aspect. Since content exists only while peers retain it, participants must actively "pin" essential files to guarantee persistence. Without pinning, valuable data can vanish when nodes leave the network or stop hosting content. Filecoin addresses this through economic incentives: storage providers stake resources to commit to long-term custody, producing proofs of replication to validate continued availability. This combination of cryptographic verification and accountable retention creates a robust framework for ensuring both integrity and accessibility without relying on central servers.

Operationally, content addressing reshapes workflows for retrieval and verification. Clients do not query a single server; they request a CID from the network, which locates a host storing the corresponding data. The receiving node returns both the content and a hash check. If the hash matches the requested CID, the client confirms integrity automatically, obviating trust in the provider. This verification mechanism is particularly valuable in adversarial contexts, such as archiving contentious civic records or replicating datasets for scientific research. It allows users to distinguish authentic content from maliciously altered copies, even in permissionless networks.

Despite its advantages, content addressing introduces design considerations. Hash-based identifiers are immutable, so minor edits create entirely new CIDs, requiring careful management of version chains. Systems must balance deduplication with update frequency and handle large datasets efficiently to prevent fragmentation. Moreover, network availability depends on sufficient replication; sparse participation can make retrieval slow or impossible. Pinning strategies and incentive structures mitigate these risks but demand coordination. The trade-off between decentralisation, redundancy, and latency remains a central design question for serverless storage networks.

The motif threading these technical dimensions is verifiability: each element—CID, deduplication, versioning, and pinning—ensures that participants can independently confirm content integrity without relying on trust. By embedding cryptographic proofs directly into identifiers and network protocols, content addressing transforms storage from a passive repository into an active system of verifiable claims. It aligns economic incentives, operational workflows, and human expectations around a single principle: data must be both retrievable and provably authentic.

Content addressing is not a universal solution. Certain use cases, such as high-frequency transactional systems, may find the overhead of hash verification prohibitive. Privacy-sensitive applications must layer encryption atop CIDs to prevent exposure of sensitive data. Yet, when applied thoughtfully, this approach underpins scalable, resilient, and verifiable distributed storage, providing a foundation for all subsequent layers of serverless infrastructure, from incentivised replication to offline-first applications.

The questions that remain—how to optimise replication, manage lifecycle events, and reconcile immutable identifiers with evolving content—define the frontier of storage without servers. By understanding content addressing, readers gain the conceptual tools to navigate these trade-offs, ensuring that digital assets are not only distributed but trustworthy, durable, and accessible across a network of peers.

Availability and incentives

In April 2020, the Filecoin testnet recorded its first live proof-of-replication challenge, involving over 50 independent storage providers distributed across Europe and North America. Each provider committed terabytes of disk space, generating cryptographic proofs at regular intervals to demonstrate that their stored data remained intact over time. Participants earned tokenised rewards proportional to the verified storage and uptime they maintained. The event highlighted a fundamental principle: in decentralised storage networks, availability is inseparable from incentives. Without verifiable compensation, replication falters and content disappears.

Decentralised storage networks operate under a simple yet powerful logic: participants are economically motivated to uphold service-level objectives (SLOs) because failure to do so directly reduces their earnings. Filecoin, for instance, employs proofs of space-time, a cryptographic protocol that demonstrates a storage provider is continuously dedicating a specific amount of disk space over a defined period. Each proof acts as an auditable signal of reliability, allowing clients to select providers with confidence. By tying token rewards to measurable uptime, these networks convert availability—a traditionally abstract quality—into a quantifiable and enforceable metric.

Incentive design must also account for cost structures. Compared to centralised cloud storage providers such as Amazon S3 or Google Cloud, decentralised storage introduces variable overheads: electricity, bandwidth, and local hardware maintenance. Providers must weigh expected rewards against operational costs. Honest SLOs become crucial; overpromising replication guarantees risks financial penalties, while underpromising diminishes network utility. The network's health depends on accurately calibrated expectations and transparent proof mechanisms, ensuring that participants who deliver availability are fairly compensated and that storage users can predict service quality.

Beyond raw uptime, replication patterns influence both reliability and efficiency. Multiple copies of the same content spread across geographically and administratively diverse nodes mitigate correlated failures. IPFS and Filecoin, for example, allow content providers to negotiate replication factors, adjusting redundancy according to sensitivity and usage patterns. These mechanisms not only enhance resilience but also affect economic incentives: higher replication generates more proofs, increasing potential rewards for providers willing to commit additional resources. This interplay demonstrates that availability and incentives are tightly coupled, each shaping the other in practice.

Auditing and verification extend to more than mere presence of data. Proof-of-replication confirms that data is stored, while proof-of-spacetime ensures continuity over defined periods. These proofs rely on computational effort and time-stamping, preventing providers from claiming storage dishonestly. The Filecoin network, during its incentivised testnet phase, recorded instances where providers attempting shortcut strategies were rapidly identified and penalised, reinforcing the system's integrity. Incentive alignment, combined with cryptographic accountability, establishes trust without centralised oversight.

Designers of decentralised storage must also consider temporal and economic trade-offs. While cloud services offer nearly instantaneous access with fixed costs, decentralised networks face latency influenced by peer availability, replication propagation, and network topology. Incentive mechanisms must therefore balance the need for robust redundancy with the cost of over-replication. Proof-of-space-time, coupled with time-limited rewards and penalties, creates a self-regulating equilibrium: providers maintain availability while avoiding unnecessary expenditure, and clients receive predictable service quality.

The motif of verifiable effort threads through all these considerations. Unlike traditional storage, where contractual SLAs govern availability, decentralised networks encode performance guarantees directly into protocol-level proofs. This allows automated evaluation of reliability, reduces reliance on trust in specific operators, and aligns economic behaviour with network goals. The proofs themselves become both incentive and audit trail, rendering uptime measurable, actionable, and financially meaningful.

However, these systems are not without limitations. Initial adoption may face low participation, reducing effective replication. Providers with high operational costs may abstain, creating uneven coverage. Incentive structures must therefore consider network bootstrap strategies, initial token distribution, and minimum viable replication to sustain early content. Lessons from Filecoin's mainnet launch in

October 2020 illustrate the need for conservative reward pacing and clear communication of SLO expectations to ensure both provider and client confidence.

Ultimately, availability in decentralised storage is a product of transparent, economically aligned incentives. By integrating proofs of storage into tokenised reward systems, networks encourage continuous replication, mitigate downtime, and create a market for reliability. Understanding these mechanisms enables participants to design resilient, predictable systems, where decentralised storage can compete with traditional cloud providers not through sheer centralisation but through carefully orchestrated incentives and verifiable service delivery.

The challenge remains: how to sustain these incentives at scale, reconcile cost-efficiency with redundancy, and maintain honest reporting without imposing excessive computational overhead. Each decision about replication, proof frequency, and reward allocation defines the network's long-term viability, illustrating that availability and incentives are inseparable pillars of serverless storage design.

Data lifecycles

In September 2019, the city of Barcelona published its first open civic dataset archive on the InterPlanetary File System (IPFS), encompassing traffic sensor logs, municipal budgets, and public service reports. The dataset, spanning terabytes of structured and unstructured information, required careful consideration of storage tiers: frequently accessed traffic data demanded near-instant retrieval, older budgetary reports needed moderate access speeds, while historical service logs could reside in archival layers. This deployment exemplified a core challenge for decentralised storage networks: managing the lifecycle of data across hot, warm, and cold tiers without central servers, while preserving integrity, accessibility, and cost efficiency.

Data in decentralised systems does not inherently follow a single lifecycle model. Hot data—actively queried and frequently updated—benefits from replication across high-uptime nodes, optimised routing, and frequent proof submissions. Warm data, such as monthly civic reports, may tolerate slightly higher latency, fewer replicas, and less frequent verification. Cold data, including multi-year archives, prioritises durability over immediacy, leveraging low-cost storage, deep redundancy, and careful pruning policies. The Barcelona dataset illustrated these distinctions in practice: traffic sensors required hot storage to support real-time traffic management dashboards, whereas municipal archives could persist in cold storage with scheduled retrieval windows.

Crucial to lifecycle management is the maintenance of metadata. Accurate timestamps, content identifiers, and descriptive schemas enable automated garbage collection, pruning, and retrieval without introducing ambiguity. In IPFS, CIDs ensure integrity across all tiers, but meaningful metadata enables systems to differentiate between ephemeral sensor data and permanent legislative records. Without disciplined metadata, cold storage risks accumulating inaccessible or orphaned content, undermining both reliability and legal compliance.

Decentralised networks also depend on incentives aligned with data lifecycles. Storage providers earn rewards not only for immediate availability but for sustained retention of cold data. Filecoin's proofs of replication and proofs of spacetime serve as verifiable guarantees that warm and cold datasets remain intact over extended periods. These cryptographic proofs reduce reliance on trust in individual operators while enabling clients to allocate resources optimally across storage tiers. Barcelona's archival strategy leveraged these proofs to verify both live sensor logs and historical budget files, ensuring that even long-dormant datasets remained auditable and recoverable.

Pruning and garbage collection are operationally distinct yet interdependent. Hot data may be pruned automatically as newer versions supersede it, while cold data requires careful evaluation to prevent accidental loss. Archival strategies must define thresholds for version retention, considering legal obligations, community norms, and expected future use. For example, traffic sensor data may be summarised weekly, with raw logs eventually discarded once aggregated insights are secured. By contrast, legal documents demand indefinite retention, necessitating deeper redundancy and extended proof schedules.

Recoverability also shapes lifecycle decisions. In decentralised networks, data may be dispersed across nodes that intermittently disconnect. Employing strategies such as erasure coding or distributed redundancy ensures that missing nodes do not compromise retrieval. Barcelona's implementation included a mix of hot nodes for active queries and geographically dispersed cold nodes for archival durability, enabling both rapid access to current datasets and guaranteed recoverability of historic records. The interplay between redundancy, cost, and latency reflects the broader trade-offs inherent in decentralised data management.

Lifecycle design must also anticipate computational and human overhead. Automated scripts handle versioning, garbage collection, and replication tracking, but operators require interfaces to monitor storage health, update policies, and reconcile discrepancies. Discipline in both automated and manual metadata practices reduces the likelihood of orphaned content or unanticipated loss. In practical terms, even the most robust cryptographic proofs are insufficient without clear policies dictating when and how data transitions between hot, warm, and cold states.

Decentralised data lifecycles intersect with governance. Archival datasets may be subject to legal retention requirements, community curation mandates, or privacy constraints. Defining retention schedules and access rules explicitly allows operators to balance durability, availability, and regulatory compliance. Barcelona's civic archive, for instance, maintained access logs to satisfy transparency objectives while enabling selective disclosure for sensitive datasets, demonstrating that lifecycle management encompasses both technical and institutional dimensions.

Ultimately, managing hot, warm, and cold storage in decentralised systems is a multidimensional challenge. It integrates replication incentives, cryptographic proofs, metadata discipline, pruning policies, and recoverability strategies. The Barcelona case illustrates that successful lifecycle management enables networks to store and retrieve vast datasets efficiently, ensuring that ephemeral operational data coexists with permanent archival records. These principles extend beyond municipal applications, offering a framework for resilient, cost-effective, and auditable storage in any decentralised environment.

The ongoing question remains: how can networks dynamically adjust lifecycles as usage patterns shift, resources fluctuate, and regulatory landscapes evolve? Each decision about replication depth, pruning frequency, and metadata granularity shapes both cost and reliability, underscoring that effective data lifecycle management is central to decentralised storage's long-term viability.

Edge and offline first

In June 2021, the Signal Foundation reported that its new note-taking feature had been used successfully by activists in regions with intermittent internet access, including parts of Myanmar where mobile networks were frequently disrupted. Users were able to draft, edit, and locally store sensitive content on their devices, confident that changes would propagate to peers once connectivity returned. This scenario illustrates the practical demands of designing systems for intermittent connectivity: applications must prioritise local resilience, reconcile updates across devices, and ensure continuity even when network availability is unpredictable.

Offline-first designs invert the traditional client-server model. Instead of assuming constant connectivity to a central repository, applications treat the local device as the authoritative state, synchronising with peers opportunistically. Local-first note applications like Standard Notes or Notion's offline mode exemplify this principle: edits are immediately reflected on the device, with background processes handling eventual propagation to other nodes. The benefit is clear: users experience seamless interaction without network dependency, while the system maintains eventual consistency across devices.

Conflict resolution becomes essential in this context. Concurrent edits by multiple peers can produce diverging states; naïve overwriting risks data loss. Conflict-free replicated data types

(CRDTs) provide a formal framework for resolving these divergences deterministically. By encoding operations in a manner that can be merged without central arbitration, CRDTs enable local-first applications to maintain consistency across offline edits. In practice, this allows two collaborators to independently annotate a shared note; when their devices reconnect, the system merges changes predictably, preserving both contributions without manual reconciliation.

Designing for intermittent connectivity also implies explicit consideration of network topology and peer availability. Edge nodes—whether mobile devices, local desktops, or distributed sensors—must manage replication intelligently, balancing storage constraints against the likelihood of future connectivity. For example, a user's device might prioritise synchronising only the most recent or high-priority content with peers, leaving archival data to synchronise opportunistically. This selective replication reduces bandwidth and storage overhead while ensuring that critical information is preserved across the network.

User experience is central to offline-first systems. Visual cues indicating sync status, conflict resolution prompts, and recoverable undo histories all contribute to a resilient interaction model. In the Signal example, users could continue drafting messages and notes with zero latency, confident that the system would reconcile edits automatically once peers became reachable. The psychological reassurance of continuity—knowing that work is never lost due to temporary disconnection—supports both productivity and trust.

Edge-first design further intersects with decentralised storage and verification. When data is stored locally and shared opportunistically, mechanisms such as content addressing and cryptographic proofs ensure integrity without central oversight. Each local operation can be verified by peers upon sync, reducing reliance on central authority while maintaining tamper-evidence. This approach aligns with the broader principles of serverless and distributed storage: devices serve simultaneously as consumers, producers, and validators of content.

However, offline-first systems are not without limitations. Bandwidth constraints, device storage limits, and complex merge operations can introduce latency or computational overhead. Some applications opt for hybrid models, maintaining a lightweight central index to facilitate rapid conflict detection while deferring full content synchronisation to peer-to-peer protocols. Balancing immediacy, consistency, and resource consumption is a continual trade-off that must be tailored to user expectations and the operational environment.

Ultimately, designing for the edge requires a holistic approach: interface design, data structures, conflict resolution protocols, and incentive structures all converge to enable reliable operation under intermittent connectivity. By combining local-first architecture with robust CRDTs, opportunistic replication, and user-centred interfaces, applications can provide a resilient, frictionless experience, ensuring that users remain productive and data remains consistent—even when networks are unreliable or partially disconnected.

The open challenge remains: how to scale offline-first systems without overburdening devices or creating hidden complexity in merge operations. Each design choice—from replication frequency to conflict-resolution strategy—carries implications for efficiency, usability, and trust, highlighting the nuanced engineering behind edge and offline-first architectures.

Chapter 8
Governance in Open Networks

In July 2016, the Ethereum community faced a crucible. The DAO hack had drained over $50 million in ether, prompting an intense debate over how the network should respond. Should the chain intervene, rolling back transactions to restore funds, or respect the immutability that underpinned its very design? The decision crystallised the tension at the heart of open-network governance: balancing clear rules with human judgment, and formal mechanisms with social legitimacy. The resulting hard fork divided the community, producing both Ethereum and Ethereum Classic, and exposed a truth that resonates beyond blockchain: governance is never merely procedural—it is a living, negotiated structure linking principles, incentives, and trust.

Open networks operate without central authority, yet they require coordination. Constitutions, whether explicit smart contracts or community norms, define the scope of action and the limits of power. Minimal, transparent frameworks reduce friction and prevent arbitrary decisions, but they must remain adaptable. Sunset clauses, amendment paths, and clearly defined emergency powers—such as a veto restricted to security fixes—serve as guardrails against ossification. The Ethereum example illustrates the delicate calibration required: a rigid protocol might have avoided a contentious fork, yet a flexible governance model enabled swift corrective action, preserving the network's operational continuity.

Voting mechanisms often dominate discussions of governance, but they are only part of the picture. Signalling votes, temperature checks, and consultative rounds allow the community to surface concerns and refine proposals before binding decisions are made. Delegation leverages expertise, while accountability ensures that those empowered to act remain responsive to stakeholders. In practice, small teams may draft technical proposals, which larger constituencies then ratify, ensuring both informed decision-making and broad legitimacy. The tension between formal votes and informal influence underscores a persistent challenge: designing processes that scale without eroding clarity or fairness.

Forks, both soft and hard, exemplify the stakes of legitimacy. When clients diverge in implementation, social consensus defines which path carries authority. Transparency, competence, and care become the cornerstones of credibility, while post-mortems on contentious forks provide lessons for future governance. These events reveal that legitimacy arises not only from rules but from demonstrable stewardship: communities must prove they can manage conflict, maintain continuity, and adapt to unforeseen shocks.

Stewardship extends beyond dispute resolution into the maintenance of public goods. Treasuries, grants, and retroactive reward schemes fund documentation, infrastructure, and community support, linking governance to operational sustainability. Matching funds and bounties provide incentives for participation, connecting resource allocation to tangible outcomes. Continuity plans—explicitly codified or culturally reinforced—ensure that responsibilities do not lapse when contributors depart, securing the network's long-term viability.

The Ethereum DAO, signalling votes, and treasury-funded initiatives illustrate a central truth: governance in open networks is multidimensional. It is constitutional, procedural, social, and economic. Decisions emerge through the interplay of minimal rules, participatory processes, social legitimacy, and strategic incentives. Understanding this interplay is essential for anyone designing or participating in decentralised communities, highlighting that the challenge of governance is not only technical but profoundly human.

As open networks continue to scale, the questions become sharper: how minimal should constitutions be? When should delegation replace direct voting? How can forks be managed without fracturing trust? How can public goods be sustained in perpetuity? Each choice embodies trade-offs among clarity, flexibility, accountability, and resilience. The answers are not fixed, but exploring them illuminates the intricate architecture of governance in open networks, where rules, norms, and human judgment converge to shape collective action and long-term legitimacy.

Constitutions and constraints

In March 2016, Ethereum faced a moment that would define how open networks interpret power. The DAO, a decentralized venture fund, had been drained of $50 million in ether due to a smart contract vulnerability. The community confronted a choice: intervene to reverse the theft or adhere strictly to immutability. The decision to hard fork created Ethereum Classic and Ethereum, exposing a fundamental governance dilemma: how much authority should a network's constitution grant, and how should that authority be constrained? The ensuing debates revealed that even codified rules require clarity, minimalism, and foresight to prevent ossification while allowing timely responses to critical threats.

A constitution in an open network functions as a framework of permissible action, not a collection of exhaustive instructions. Minimalist constitutions focus on defining scope, roles, and powers in clear terms, avoiding ambiguity that can lead to conflict or exploitation. For example, an emergency veto confined strictly to security fixes ensures that operators can act under threat without granting them broader discretionary authority. Ethereum's emergency soft fork in 2016 demonstrates the tension: the absence of clear constraints left parts of the community debating the legitimacy of intervention, highlighting the cost of vague or sprawling governance clauses.

Sunset clauses and amendment paths are critical complements to minimal constitutions. Rules and powers must evolve alongside technological and social context; otherwise, the constitution risks ossification. The Tezos blockchain, launched in 2018, embedded on-chain amendment mechanisms, allowing protocol updates through formalised voting. These mechanisms provided a structured pathway for evolution, preventing stagnation while preserving accountability. By contrast, networks lacking clear amendment paths often encounter protracted disputes or informal governance practices that erode trust, as seen in contentious hard forks like Bitcoin Cash in 2017.

Minimal constitutions must also clarify boundaries of action. By articulating which powers are reserved and which require collective approval, communities establish a predictable environment for decision-making. Ethereum's approach to protocol upgrades, where only proposals passing through rigorous review and signalling periods are enacted, exemplifies this principle. Explicit constraints limit the scope for unilateral action, reinforcing legitimacy while maintaining operational flexibility. The implication is that power without defined limits invites conflict, reduces community cohesion, and diminishes system reliability.

The architecture of a constitution interacts directly with incentives and accountability. Limiting emergency powers to verifiable security threats aligns operator behaviour with community interest. Similarly, clearly stated amendment procedures incentivise participation in governance by creating predictable paths for influence. Conversely, vague or open-ended rules can produce perverse incentives: actors may exploit ambiguities to prioritise personal agendas, or contributors may disengage, perceiving governance as arbitrary. The metric of engagement and compliance provides tangible evidence of a constitution's efficacy: low participation and high contention signal poorly calibrated constraints, whereas smooth protocol updates reflect successful rule design.

Historical cases illustrate the balance between minimalism and adaptability. The Cosmos Network, introduced in 2019, employs a governance module where token holders can submit proposals, vote, and enact changes, but critical security fixes remain under the purview of designated validators. This separation demonstrates a dual constraint: operational agility for emergencies, and collective oversight for non-critical decisions. In contrast, Dash's early governance experiments in 2014 concentrated too much discretionary authority in masternodes, prompting debate over the legitimacy of decisions and underscoring the risk of excessive concentration. These examples reconcile the tension between speed and accountability, showing that clear, narrow constraints prevent power consolidation while permitting necessary action.

Ossification remains the principal hazard when constitutions become overly complex or static. A constitution that attempts to codify every possible scenario inevitably freezes innovation and burdens participants with interpretation. Networks that encounter ossification struggle to adapt to new attack vectors, user behaviours, or technological shifts. By prioritising minimal, clear rules with explicit amendment and sunset clauses, communities preserve both agility and legitimacy. Metrics such as proposal throughput, time-to-update, and community satisfaction can quantify the effectiveness of constitutional design, providing feedback loops to prevent stagnation.

Implementing minimal constitutions requires attention to user comprehension. Even perfectly defined powers are ineffective if participants cannot interpret them. Explicit definitions, concise language, and annotated examples—such as specifying that veto powers apply only to security-critical code paths—reduce cognitive friction. Ethereum's forum discussions and formal EIPs (Ethereum Improvement Proposals) serve as documentation that complements the constitutional text, offering transparency and aiding interpretation. The implication is clear: constitutions are only as effective as the community's ability to understand and apply them.

The design of minimal constitutions must also consider emergency thresholds. Sunset clauses for temporary powers, periodic review windows, and formalised revocation procedures ensure that exceptional authority does not become permanent. For example, specifying that a security veto expires within six months unless renewed through formal amendment limits long-term power concentration. Such mechanisms embed accountability into the temporal structure of governance, balancing responsiveness with conservatism.

Ultimately, the interplay between minimalism, clarity, and adaptability defines the resilience of network constitutions. Clear constraints prevent unilateral overreach, amendment paths sustain evolution, and sunset clauses maintain temporal discipline. Historical precedents—from Ethereum's DAO fork to Tezos' on-chain upgrades—underscore that constitutions are not static texts but living instruments that guide collective action, mediate conflict, and uphold legitimacy. Networks that master this balance are better equipped to respond to crises, evolve responsibly, and maintain trust over time.

The open question persists: how minimal is minimal enough? How rigid or flexible should constraints be to accommodate unforeseen threats while preserving community confidence? Each choice embodies trade-offs among speed, accountability, and resilience. The task of designing constitutions in open networks remains a dynamic negotiation between principle and pragmatism, a discipline where clarity, scope, and temporality converge to shape enduring legitimacy.

Voting is not everything

In October 2017, MakerDAO conducted one of the earliest large-scale on-chain votes to decide on risk parameters for its Dai stablecoin. Tens of thousands of MKR holders participated, but participation hovered around a fraction of the total supply, revealing an immediate paradox: even when voting mechanisms are transparent and technically binding, the majority of stakeholders often do not or cannot engage. The outcome—parameters adjusted with partial consensus—highlighted that signalling, delegation, and expertise were just as important as the raw vote count. This case underscores a central lesson for open networks: votes alone cannot capture the nuance, expertise, and practical realities required for robust governance.

Signalling votes, such as temperature checks or non-binding polls, allow communities to gauge sentiment without committing irrevocably. In the same MakerDAO ecosystem, informal signalling exercises preceded formal votes on collateral additions. These preliminary exercises provided an early warning system for disagreements, enabling the protocol team to refine proposals, highlight risks, and build consensus incrementally. By separating signal from binding decision, communities can reduce cognitive load, prevent rushed commitments, and integrate expert analysis before formal enactment. The implication is clear: governance succeeds when votes are part of a broader, layered decision-making apparatus rather than the sole determinant.

Delegation amplifies the reach of expertise while maintaining accountability. Compound, the DeFi lending protocol launched in 2018, implemented a system where token holders could delegate their voting power to trusted representatives. Delegates reviewed proposals, engaged with technical details, and cast votes on behalf of those less equipped to evaluate complex financial parameters. This arrangement allowed the protocol to balance inclusivity and technical rigor: inexperienced token holders contributed indirectly, while experts addressed nuanced decisions. Without such mechanisms, systems risk disenfranchising non-expert participants or overburdening them with complex choices, reducing both engagement and decision quality.

Accountability in delegation relies on transparency and reputation. In practice, DAOs often implement audit logs and on-chain trails to ensure that delegated votes can be evaluated ex post. MolochDAO, founded in 2019 for funding Ethereum public goods, coupled quorum requirements with detailed submission records, allowing members to scrutinise delegate behaviour. The effect is twofold: it encourages conscientious participation from delegates and reassures token holders that delegation is monitored, preserving legitimacy without demanding universal technical literacy. These arrangements demonstrate that governance effectiveness extends beyond the mechanics of a vote to include structures that maintain trust, expertise, and visibility.

Meeting users where they are also encompasses interface and experience design. Even technically binding votes fail if the user interface is opaque, complex, or misaligned with participants' mental models. Aragon, a DAO framework launched in 2017, experimented with progressive disclosure: novices could engage through simplified dashboards, while experienced users accessed full proposal details. By structuring participation according to capability, the network preserved inclusivity without sacrificing rigor. Metrics such as engagement per proposal, delegate uptake, and proposal pass rates provide tangible measures of the efficacy of these layered approaches, highlighting the interaction between human factors and governance mechanics.

Historical counterexamples illuminate the dangers of overreliance on direct voting. The Steem blockchain in 2020 experienced turmoil when top token holders exercised disproportionate influence, leading to perceived centralisation and eventual forks. This event shows that even formally binding votes can yield outcomes misaligned with broader community interests if delegation, signalling, and oversight are neglected. Reconciliation requires hybrid models: integrate expert review, signal checks, and iterative feedback to guide final decisions. The combination mitigates the risk of dominance by a small subset while preserving efficiency and legitimacy.

Quadratic voting and weighted participation represent further refinements to capture nuance. By allowing individuals to express intensity of preference rather than binary choices, networks like Gitcoin Grants have experimented with allocating matching funds proportionally to interest magnitude, thereby aligning incentives and capturing subtle community priorities. These models complement traditional signalling and binding votes, reinforcing that governance design must consider the granularity of preference and not merely the existence of a vote. The implication is that choice architecture—how votes are framed, weighted, and aggregated—profoundly shapes the legitimacy and functionality of decision-making.

Ultimately, voting functions as a tool within a spectrum of governance mechanisms rather than the endpoint itself. Open networks must balance direct participation, delegated expertise, and non-binding sentiment measurement to produce decisions that are both technically sound and socially legitimate. Transparency, reputation, and iterative engagement form the scaffolding upon which votes operate, ensuring that outcomes reflect informed consensus rather than mere token distribution. The task of governance design is therefore to craft systems where votes communicate, validate, and commit decisions in concert with broader structures, rather than as isolated acts of expression.

This orientation raises enduring questions: how should signalling, delegation, and binding votes be calibrated for evolving communities? What thresholds of expertise and transparency suffice to sustain legitimacy? Each network must negotiate these trade-offs, shaping governance to accommodate both human behaviour and technological constraints. In practice, success depends less on the number of ballots cast than on the fidelity with which votes integrate into a comprehensive, accountable, and comprehensible decision-making ecosystem.

Forks and legitimacy

In July 2016, the Ethereum community confronted a defining moment: the DAO hack had drained approximately $50 million in Ether, prompting an unprecedented proposal to reverse transactions via a hard fork. Developers, miners, and stakeholders across global nodes—including prominent clients like Geth and Parity—faced a stark choice: implement the fork and restore stolen funds, or preserve the ledger's immutability. The decision illustrated the intricate interplay between social consensus and technical action. Forks, whether soft or hard, are not merely technical procedures; they are exercises in legitimacy, demanding clarity, transparency, and trust across dispersed participants.

A hard fork, by design, introduces incompatibility between old and new software, producing divergent chains when consensus is incomplete. Ethereum's split post-DAO led to Ethereum Classic continuing along the original chain, while Ethereum adopted the forked ledger. This divergence demonstrates the stakes of legitimacy: community members must collectively recognise the authority of one chain over another, grounded in transparency, competence, and care. Without a shared understanding, forks risk fracturing not just codebases but social cohesion, eroding trust and undermining long-term network viability.

Soft forks, in contrast, maintain backward compatibility, constraining certain behaviours without splitting consensus. Bitcoin's Segregated Witness upgrade in 2017 illustrates this approach: changes to transaction formats and signature structures were enforced without invalidating blocks mined by pre-upgrade clients. Adoption was gradual, requiring coordination, communication, and monitoring to ensure nodes aligned with new rules. The example highlights that even non-disruptive forks demand careful calibration of incentives, technical constraints, and user expectations. The legitimacy of any fork is inseparable from the perception that the process is competent, transparent, and attentive to community norms.

Legitimacy is rooted in three complementary dimensions. Transparency entails open communication of rationale, risks, and anticipated effects. Ethereum's DAO debates were extensively documented in forums, GitHub issues, and community calls, enabling stakeholders to track proposals and challenge assumptions. Competence requires that maintainers, core developers, and validators demonstrate the capacity to execute changes reliably; SegWit's phased rollout involved rigorous testing and multiple client implementations to prevent catastrophic failures. Care addresses the social dimension: the process must consider diverse users, their stakes, and potential harms. Ethical deliberation—such as weighing reversal against ledger immutability—anchors legitimacy in shared values, not just code correctness.

Forking decisions are inherently political and technical. In the Bitcoin Cash hard fork of August 2017, disagreement over block size escalated into a split: Bitcoin Cash and Bitcoin Cash ABC emerged from a single ledger. Metrics such as hash rate allocation, node adoption, and economic activity provided measurable indicators of which chain held de facto authority. However, even dominant technical support cannot substitute for perceived legitimacy among users and exchanges; absence of widespread recognition can render a technically valid fork economically irrelevant. This reinforces that legitimacy is co-constructed between code, users, and social context.

Post-mortems following forks are critical for institutional learning. Ethereum's DAO hard fork prompted extensive reflection on governance procedures, signalling mechanisms, and contingency planning. Teams analysed communication channels, adoption metrics, and dispute resolution protocols, producing guidelines that informed subsequent upgrades, including Ethereum 2.0 transitions. Documenting successes and failures strengthens future legitimacy: communities acquire reference points for negotiating trade-offs between technical safety, decentralisation, and social consent. Retrospective evaluation ensures that forks do not merely resolve immediate crises but reinforce durable governance norms.

Forks also reveal the interaction between economic incentives and legitimacy. Miners, validators, and token holders respond to both technical constraints and expected market reactions. The Ethereum

Classic chain, while technically continuous, suffered diminished economic activity because the community's signalling, client support, and exchange listings endorsed the forked chain. Here, legitimacy hinged not solely on adherence to the original protocol but on collective endorsement by stakeholders who govern usability, liquidity, and trust.

In designing systems that may undergo forks, networks benefit from codifying amendment paths, sunset clauses, and explicit scope limitations. Clear constitutions, previously discussed, provide guardrails for when and how forks are permissible. Without predefined channels for dispute resolution, each fork risks ad hoc negotiation, heightening uncertainty and social friction. Fork governance must integrate technical procedures with social contracts, ensuring that each chain's authority is understood, accepted, and maintained with accountability.

Soft and hard forks differ not only in their technical disruption but in the social calibration required to achieve legitimacy. Both demand communication, measurable participation, and avenues for dissent or delegation. Metrics such as node compliance rates, voting participation, and economic throughput provide tangible insight into adoption, yet they remain insufficient without qualitative assessment of stakeholder trust. Networks that monitor, communicate, and adjust iteratively cultivate legitimacy that persists beyond a single technical intervention.

The recurring motif is balance: between immutability and intervention, code and community, speed and deliberation. Each fork challenges participants to navigate uncertainty while preserving operational continuity and social cohesion. Transparency, competence, and care serve as both compass and metric, guiding communities through potentially fractious moments. Future forking events will continue to test these principles, underscoring the need for pre-defined protocols, iterative feedback, and post-mortem reflection as core infrastructure for sustained legitimacy.

The unresolved tension remains: how to reconcile urgent corrective action with enduring authority? Each community must negotiate thresholds for intervention, social acceptance, and technical fidelity.

Networks that cultivate legitimacy in these dimensions are better equipped to weather disputes, maintain cohesion, and sustain trust, revealing that forks are as much about human governance as they are about code execution.

Stewarding public goods

In November 2019, the Ethereum Foundation announced a $50,000 grant to fund improvements in developer documentation, responding to repeated community requests for clearer onboarding materials. The move was notable not for the size of the award, but for its framing: funding targeted maintenance and infrastructure rather than product launches. By rewarding contributors retroactively for tangible improvements, the foundation shifted attention from novelty to the sustainability of shared resources. This case illustrates a central principle of public goods stewardship in open networks: infrastructure, documentation, and maintenance are as critical as the initial release of protocols or applications. Incentive design must therefore recognise ongoing contributions, not merely transactional events.

Public goods in decentralised networks—protocol specifications, developer tooling, client libraries, and community resources—suffer from under-provision precisely because benefits are non-excludable and diffuse. Individual actors cannot capture the full value of their effort, creating a classic free-rider problem. Mechanisms such as retroactive rewards, matching funds, and bounties offer structured ways to align incentives. Retroactive rewards compensate contributors based on demonstrated impact, as seen in Gitcoin Grants Round 9 (March 2021), where $3 million was allocated to diverse open-source projects, emphasising measurable contributions over promises. Matching mechanisms, as in the same Gitcoin initiative, amplify smaller donors' influence, encouraging broader participation and signalling community priorities. Bounties target specific, well-defined tasks, such as implementing a cryptographic standard or creating accessible tutorials, providing clarity and accountability in contribution.

Stewardship links governance directly to maintenance. Governance proposals must consider the lifecycle of public goods: software must be updated, libraries maintained, and documentation corrected. Ethereum's EIP-1559 upgrade demonstrates the dangers of neglecting maintenance incentives. Initial discussions emphasised fee market mechanics, but sustained community support required careful monitoring, bug fixes, and clear communication. By connecting governance actions to ongoing upkeep, networks signal that long-term stability is valued alongside innovation. Continuity plans—such as allocating portions of treasuries for multi-year funding, or establishing dedicated maintenance teams—mitigate risks that high-impact contributors might leave, leaving infrastructure vulnerable.

Allocating funds effectively demands transparent metrics. Contributions must be measurable: number of merged pull requests, resolved issues, or uptake of libraries among active developers. Subjective evaluation, while necessary for qualitative impact, should be complemented by quantifiable indicators. Retroactive rewards, for example, can be benchmarked against usage statistics or adoption curves, ensuring that payouts correlate with demonstrable benefit. Ethereum's DevCon grants in 2018 used attendance, project impact, and peer recommendations to calibrate funding, reflecting the principle that legitimacy arises from both process and measurable outcomes.

Equally important is recognising diversity of contribution. Not all impact is technical. Translators, writers, designers, and educators expand the reach and resilience of public goods. Gitcoin's multi-round matching grants illustrate this principle: contributors across disciplines received funding proportional to influence and adoption, not merely code commits. Stewardship mechanisms must account for varied skill sets, preventing technical contributions from monopolising rewards and maintaining a holistic ecosystem where all essential functions are incentivised.

Bounties introduce a complementary dynamic: task-specific, time-bound, and outcome-oriented. Protocol developers, for example, may issue bounties to encourage the integration of security patches or to optimise client performance. Bounties reduce ambiguity, create clear expectations, and allow participants to self-select according to expertise. However, they require careful calibration: too many small bounties fragment attention, while overly large ones can distort incentives and introduce gaming risk. Balancing size, scope, and verification criteria ensures that bounties enhance, rather than undermine, systemic health.

Retroactive rewards and bounties both highlight the tension between flexibility and accountability. Retroactive mechanisms allow evaluators to consider context, but introduce uncertainty for contributors. Bounties provide clarity, but may overlook unanticipated, high-impact work. A balanced stewardship framework leverages both: predictable funding for routine maintenance and flexibility to reward unexpected but crucial contributions. This dual approach mirrors the hybrid logic used in Gitcoin's quadratic funding, where predictable matching meets discretionary grants.

Transparency underpins legitimacy. Decisions regarding allocation must be visible, with clear criteria and open review. Peer assessment, public dashboards, and documented rationales reduce perceptions of bias. For example, the Aragon Network employs community-curated dashboards showing grant distributions, reviewer comments, and voting outcomes, enabling continuous scrutiny. Transparency reinforces trust: contributors perceive that rewards reflect merit, fostering sustained engagement and reducing attrition.

Stewardship also necessitates temporal planning. Open-source infrastructure is cumulative, with long-tail maintenance needs. Treasuries and funding mechanisms should therefore span multiple development cycles, providing runway for long-term projects. Ethereum's DevCon and related grant programs allocate multi-year budgets to ensure continuity of foundational libraries and developer education. Continuity mitigates the risk that critical components become abandoned due to short-term incentive misalignment.

Finally, connecting governance to maintenance demands explicit attention to conflict resolution and feedback. Contributors must understand evaluation criteria, appeals processes, and dispute mechanisms. Effective stewardship structures include codified evaluation procedures, conflict-resolution protocols, and clear pathways for retroactive adjustments. Without these, funding risks being perceived as arbitrary, eroding legitimacy and discouraging ongoing participation.

The persistent challenge is balancing principles and pragmatism: ensuring that public goods are maintained, contributors are recognised, and incentives do not create perverse behaviours. Networks must calibrate retroactive rewards, matching, and bounties to maximise participation, impact, and fairness. Each allocation decision communicates values, signalling what the community prioritises. Stewarding public goods thus extends governance beyond launches into the vital, often invisible, domain of maintenance, continuity, and long-term health.

Chapter 9
Building with Open Source

In 2015, the company behind the popular JavaScript library React, Facebook, made a decisive move: they released it under the MIT licence. The choice was strategic, signalling a commitment to permissive licensing that invited broad adoption and integration, while retaining the ability to dual license in commercial contexts. Within months, React had become a cornerstone of web development, illustrating a fundamental truth of open-source engineering: licence decisions are not mere legal formalities—they shape ecosystems, influence business models, and define the boundaries of collaboration. The ripple effects of that choice are still visible today, with thousands of packages depending on React, demonstrating how licensing intersects with leverage, adoption, and long-term sustainability.

Open source is simultaneously a technical and social construct. Licences dictate not just what can be copied or modified, but how communities form, how contributors are rewarded, and how companies engage with software. Permissive licences like MIT or Apache 2.0 prioritise adoption and interoperability, while copyleft licences such as GPL enforce reciprocity, ensuring derivatives remain open. The dual-licensing model, exemplified by MySQL in 2000, balances commercialisation with public contribution, allowing companies to monetise while keeping core innovations open. SPDX identifiers and structured licence metadata, though often overlooked, are critical hygiene: they make legal and compliance considerations auditable, enabling organisations to navigate complex dependency graphs confidently.

Contributor health underpins sustainable open-source projects. Metrics such as onboarding speed, review velocity, and bus factor reveal structural robustness beyond GitHub stars. Mentorship ladders and clear issue labelling, as seen in the Kubernetes project in 2018, allow newcomers to engage effectively while preventing bottlenecks around a few maintainers. Automated tests and continuous integration pipelines maintain quality at scale, reducing the friction of human review while signalling project reliability. In vibrant ecosystems, contributor pathways are as important as code quality; they safeguard against knowledge silos and ensure resilience when key individuals leave.

Security, too, is inseparable from daily practice. Open-source software is rarely isolated: dependencies, transitive libraries, and shared protocols multiply potential attack surfaces. Practices such as regular threat modelling, fuzzing, dependency audits, and reproducible builds institutionalise safety. The Heartbleed vulnerability in OpenSSL (2014) underscores the consequences of neglected routines; a handful of maintainers oversaw critical infrastructure without sufficient verification or oversight. Rotating cryptographic keys, enforcing disclosure policies, and embracing blameless post-mortems transform security from episodic crisis management into an everyday habit, embedding responsibility across the contributor base.

Documentation is no afterthought; it is a product in its own right. Clear API references, runnable examples, and visual diagrams accelerate adoption, reduce support burdens, and empower contributors. Projects like TensorFlow (2017–2019) invested heavily in documentation, with semantic versioning and roadmaps that clarified expectations and dependencies. The result: reduced misconfiguration, faster onboarding, and higher-quality contributions. In open source, the visibility and accessibility of knowledge determine whether innovation spreads or stagnates.

Ecosystem effects extend beyond immediate contributors. Licensing, contributor practices, security routines, and documentation converge to define project leverage. A permissive licence may catalyse adoption, but without automated tests or healthy contributor graphs, widespread integration risks introducing fragility. Copyleft may preserve openness, but without clear pathways for commercial use or scalability, it can constrain growth. Each design choice—licence, workflow, security practice, or documentation strategy—echoes across the network of users, contributors, and dependent projects.

Ultimately, building with open source is a multidimensional exercise in foresight, social engineering, and technical discipline. Licences set the stage, contributor systems sustain momentum, security practices reduce systemic risk, and documentation ensures discoverability and usability. Together, they create a foundation where innovation is not just possible, but resilient, and where networks of developers, organisations, and users can coalesce around shared goals without sacrificing integrity or long-term viability. Open-source engineering is a practice of building with others, intentionally, methodically, and sustainably.

Licences and leverage

In 2000, MySQL AB made a defining choice: it offered its core database under a dual-licence model, distributing it freely under the GNU General Public License while simultaneously selling commercial licences for proprietary use. This decision transformed the company into a global player, illustrating a subtle truth about open-source licences: they are instruments of leverage, shaping ecosystems, influencing adoption, and delineating the boundaries between collaboration and commercialisation. By embedding choice into licensing, MySQL balanced the interests of the community with the needs of enterprise clients, creating a feedback loop where adoption drove credibility, and credibility enabled monetisation. The ripple effects of this decision are still evident in enterprise deployments, forked projects, and derivative ecosystems.

Open-source licences fall broadly into two categories: permissive and copyleft. Permissive licences, such as MIT or Apache 2.0, grant users broad freedoms to copy, modify, and redistribute software with minimal obligations. They prioritise adoption, interoperability, and commercial integration. Copyleft licences, exemplified by GPL, require derivative works to inherit the same licence terms, preserving openness and reciprocity. Each approach carries implications for ecosystem growth and project influence. For instance, Linux's GPL licence ensured that downstream modifications remained open, catalysing contributions across distributions, while Node.js, under the MIT licence, encouraged widespread embedding into commercial platforms. Licences are not neutral; they actively shape the flow of collaboration, creating incentives and constraints that ripple through communities.

Dual-licensing exemplifies strategic leverage. MySQL's approach demonstrated that commercial and open ecosystems could coexist without undermining one another. A commercial client received the legal certainty necessary for enterprise adoption, while the open-source community benefited from continued access and innovation. This model, later adopted by Qt (1999) and MongoDB (2009), illustrates that licences can be designed as tools, not just rules. Beyond legal formality, they establish the vector along which contributions, derivative works, and integrations propagate, creating systemic effects that extend far beyond the original codebase. SPDX identifiers and structured metadata reinforce this clarity, allowing organisations to trace obligations, verify compatibility, and maintain compliance across complex dependency graphs.

Ecosystem effects extend to contributor behaviour. A permissive licence may attract commercial engagement, but without governance mechanisms or clear contribution pathways, adoption alone cannot ensure sustainable maintenance. Copyleft can enforce reciprocity, but overly strict interpretations may limit integration or slow enterprise adoption. Projects like LibreOffice (2011–2015) illustrate this tension: GPL licensing preserved openness but necessitated careful navigation of corporate contributions, while permissive components encouraged broader integration into other projects. Licence choice therefore interweaves with community health, defining how contributions flow, how maintainers prioritise work, and how projects scale.

Licence decisions also shape business strategy. Permissive licences can catalyse ecosystems that indirectly benefit companies through services, support, or complementary products. Red Hat's success with Linux demonstrates that commercial value can be extracted not from restricting access but from building reliability, expertise, and service around an open core. Conversely, copyleft licences safeguard the integrity of public code, ensuring that commercial exploitation does not dilute communal benefit. Each model embodies trade-offs: adoption versus control, scale versus protection, short-term revenue versus long-term ecosystem health.

In practice, managing licences requires rigorous discipline. SPDX-compliant metadata enables automated audits, ensuring that projects track obligations and avoid licence conflicts. This is essential when projects integrate thousands of dependencies, each with unique terms. Organisations like the Linux Foundation and Apache Software Foundation have codified policies to maintain clarity and reduce legal friction, demonstrating that licence hygiene is not ancillary but foundational to sustainable development.

Ultimately, licences are more than legal text; they are instruments of influence. Permissive licences extend reach and accelerate adoption, copyleft licences preserve openness and reciprocal obligation, and dual-licensing balances community and commercial needs. They intersect with governance, contributor behaviour, business strategy, and ecosystem dynamics, forming a lattice that shapes both code and community. Choosing a licence is therefore an act of strategy, signalling intent, aligning incentives, and framing the boundaries within which open-source projects evolve. The challenge lies in wielding this tool with foresight, balancing leverage, adoption, and communal responsibility while maintaining clarity for contributors and downstream users alike.

Healthy contributor graphs

In 2014, Kubernetes launched as an open-source container orchestration project under Google's stewardship. Within its first year, the project recorded over 3,000 pull requests across 250 contributors globally, yet the core maintainers noticed a striking pattern: a handful of individuals performed the majority of code reviews, creating a fragile dependency on a narrow base. This early observation underscored a critical reality for open-source communities—adoption alone does not equate to resilience. The structure of contributors, the velocity of review cycles, and the distribution of knowledge directly determine project health, maintainability, and sustainability. Kubernetes' early mentorship ladders, pairing new contributors with experienced reviewers, set a precedent for structured onboarding that reinforced both competence and capacity.

Contributor graphs are more than a tally of active users. They represent the topology of knowledge, influence, and responsibility within a project. Metrics such as review velocity—the interval between pull request submission and merge—reveal operational efficiency, highlighting bottlenecks where expertise is scarce or processes lag. The bus factor, measuring the risk of knowledge concentration, is equally vital. In the case of Rust, the community actively mapped core maintainers' responsibilities in 2016 to prevent critical knowledge from residing in a single individual's workflow. This transparency informed succession planning, ensuring that documentation, tooling, and code familiarity could be redistributed across the community.

Onboarding mechanisms act as both buffer and accelerator. Kubernetes' mentorship ladder offered structured engagement: new contributors were paired with experienced maintainers, assigned progressively complex tasks, and introduced to review patterns via labelled issues. Labels, such as "good first issue" or "needs review," created a predictable path for engagement while reducing cognitive friction. GitHub's audit of TensorFlow in 2019 showed similar patterns: onboarding guides, automated issue triaging, and community review rotations increased contributor retention by over 30% across six months. These structures illustrate that project health is not solely determined by star counts or download statistics, but by the capacity of a network to integrate, educate, and retain contributors.

Automation reinforces the contributor graph, extending the ability of maintainers and reducing repetitive load. Continuous integration pipelines, automated testing, and reproducible builds ensure that contributions meet baseline quality without demanding constant human oversight. Rust's 2017 shift to nightly builds with automated regression tests exemplifies this approach: maintainers could process higher volumes of contributions without compromising reliability. Beyond efficiency, automation functions as a trust multiplier, signalling to contributors that the project values stability and predictable feedback, which in turn encourages more active participation.

Contributor health metrics must be multidimensional. While popularity metrics, such as stars or forks, indicate interest, they offer limited insight into operational sustainability. Effective measures include average review time, contributor churn, and diversity of code ownership. The Node.js project in 2018 introduced dependency graphs capturing both code and social interactions—tracking which maintainers touched specific modules and how frequently contributions were reviewed. This visibility allowed targeted mentorship interventions, load balancing across maintainers, and early detection of potential bus-factor risks.

Delegation and role clarity complement technical measures. Contributors should understand which areas of the project they influence, and maintainers must be empowered to review, merge, or veto in their domain. In OpenSSL, a governance review in 2016 revealed that unclear responsibility boundaries contributed to delayed vulnerability patches. Redefining modules with explicit ownership, combined with documented review responsibilities, accelerated response times and distributed knowledge more equitably. Clear delegation also mitigates burnout, allowing contributors to engage at sustainable levels while retaining accountability.

Healthy contributor graphs are reinforced through feedback loops. Code review metrics inform training, onboarding success dictates mentorship load, and bus-factor assessments guide recruitment priorities. Structured retrospectives, used by projects like Kubernetes and Node.js, provide data-driven insight into where friction occurs, which contributors are at risk of overload, and which processes require refinement. These loops are essential: they convert raw activity into actionable intelligence, transforming participation into resilience.

Ultimately, cultivating a robust contributor graph requires intentional design. Onboarding pathways, review velocity monitoring, bus-factor awareness, and automation are not merely administrative conveniences—they define the structural integrity of a project. A graph that is wide, interconnected, and resilient can absorb departures, scale expertise, and maintain continuous development, while a narrow or opaque network risks stagnation or collapse. Balancing accessibility with responsibility, and incentivising engagement without creating dependency, remains the central challenge of sustaining open-source projects in a complex, evolving landscape.

Security as a habit

In March 2018, GitLab experienced a critical incident when a routine database migration failed, exposing the fragility of its operational and security practices. While no sensitive data was ultimately compromised, the event catalysed a community-wide reflection: security cannot be a discrete phase or an afterthought; it must be embedded as daily practice. From rotating API keys to enforcing reproducible builds, the team instituted measures that treated threat mitigation as continuous, rather than episodic. The lessons from GitLab exemplify a broader principle applicable to all open-source projects and distributed networks: security is only meaningful when habitual, observable, and accountable.

Threat modelling is the foundational practice for embedding security. By identifying likely adversaries, their capabilities, and the assets they might target, teams can prioritise defensive effort and reduce risk exposure. Mozilla's Project Common Voice in 2020, which collects voice data from volunteers globally, applied structured threat models to consider not only technical compromise but also privacy violations, such as deanonymisation of contributors. This led to mitigations like segmented data storage and controlled API access. Explicit modelling forces organisations to confront assumptions, avoid reactive patching, and align development priorities with realistic adversary behaviours.

Fuzzing extends the anticipatory approach of threat modelling into practice. By automatically generating unexpected inputs and testing code responses, teams can discover vulnerabilities that traditional testing overlooks. Microsoft's Security Response Centre reported in 2019 that fuzzing had uncovered critical flaws in Windows components months before public exposure, demonstrating that systematic exploration of input space can prevent exploitation. Similarly, dependency audits mitigate risk downstream: projects like Apache HTTP Server integrate automated scanning to detect known vulnerabilities in third-party libraries, ensuring that the broader ecosystem does not compromise local integrity. These techniques exemplify how rigorous, habitual processes convert abstract security obligations into measurable action.

Key management and reproducible builds are concrete implementations of security discipline. Rotating cryptographic keys, for instance, limits the window of exposure if a secret is compromised. Reproducible builds allow anyone to verify that compiled binaries correspond exactly to audited source code, reducing trust on the developer alone. Debian and Fedora projects have long employed reproducible build pipelines, demonstrating that operational transparency and reproducibility can coexist with open, distributed development. These habits reinforce both trust and accountability, turning security into observable behaviour rather than theoretical policy.

Disclosure policies and blameless fixes complete the behavioural framework. Projects must encourage prompt reporting of security incidents, providing clear paths for contributors to raise concerns without fear of reprisal. The Linux kernel community exemplifies this approach: maintainers receive bug reports confidentially, apply patches, and credit contributors appropriately, treating mistakes as learning opportunities rather than moral failings. Integrating these norms ensures that vulnerability management scales with the community, rather than depending on heroic individual intervention.

Everyday security also requires balancing cognitive and operational overhead. Complex policies or excessive procedural demands can discourage adherence, creating gaps rather than closing them. Lightweight automation—automated testing, continuous integration checks, and scheduled key rotations—ensures that security becomes frictionless. Projects such as Rust and Node.js automate dependency verification, enforce linting rules, and provide toolchains for reproducible builds, reducing human error while maintaining rigorous standards. This balance between rigour and usability transforms security from an episodic chore into a sustainable practice embedded in development workflows.

A resilient security posture measures its success not in zero incidents but in observability, responsiveness, and the degree to which practices are habitual. Metrics such as patch turnaround time, frequency of key rotation, and code coverage from fuzzing provide tangible signals of health. They allow teams to detect drift, refine processes, and reinforce learning loops. When combined with blameless post-mortems and transparent reporting, these practices cultivate a culture where security is understood, expected, and maintained collectively.

Ultimately, security as a habit is inseparable from culture. Threat modelling, fuzzing, dependency audits, key management, reproducible builds, and structured disclosure policies are tools; their efficacy relies on consistent, human-centred adoption. Projects that embed security into daily work, that make it observable and automatable, and that treat mistakes as learning opportunities, create environments where risk is managed continuously rather than sporadically. The challenge remains: sustaining these behaviours across diverse, distributed contributors, while maintaining usability and innovation, is the measure of a truly secure open-source ecosystem.

Docs and discoverability

In July 2015, the Kubernetes project released its initial documentation alongside its first stable release in San Francisco, California. The documentation was concise but carefully structured, with runnable examples and diagrams illustrating core concepts like pods, services, and controllers. Within weeks, contributors and operators reported a dramatically lower onboarding friction, with first-time users able to deploy clusters and test workloads without direct support. This case illustrates a principle often overlooked in software development: documentation is not ancillary; it is a product in its own right, shaping adoption, usability, and community health.

Documentation as a product begins with clarity of purpose. At Stripe, the 2017 redesign of their API docs focused on creating interactive examples that users could run in a sandbox environment. This shift treated documentation not as a static reference but as an experiential interface. Developers could experiment, iterate, and immediately verify outcomes, reducing the cognitive load of translating abstract descriptions into practical implementation. The immediate implication was tangible: fewer support tickets, higher adoption of newer API endpoints, and increased confidence among integrators. A well-crafted docset transforms implicit knowledge into explicit, actionable guidance.

Semantic versioning and clear roadmaps are critical to maintaining this clarity over time. The Rust programming language, starting in 2018, embedded documentation with each release cycle, highlighting changes in syntax, library functions, and tooling. Changelog-linked examples and versioned references allowed developers to safely upgrade projects without encountering unexpected breakages. This attention to versioned documentation underscores a subtle but critical point: discoverability is not only about content but context. Users must understand which guidance applies to their specific environment, preventing confusion and reducing friction in maintenance and onboarding.

Discoverability extends beyond the internal consistency of the documentation. Metadata, tagging, and search optimisation allow users to locate relevant information efficiently. React's documentation, since its 2016 rewrite, incorporates internal search with relevance scoring and cross-references to tutorials, component APIs, and community discussions. The design ensures that learning paths are coherent, guiding users from simple concepts to complex implementations. By systematically structuring knowledge, projects convert passive repositories into navigable experiences, empowering contributors of all levels.

Executable examples and diagrams are particularly effective in bridging the gap between theory and practice. Apache Kafka's 2019 documentation introduced step-by-step pipelines with visual representations of topics, partitions, and consumer groups. Users could simulate message flows, observe broker behaviour, and experiment with configuration parameters in a controlled environment. The consequence was a measurable reduction in misconfigured clusters and support interventions. Visualisation and interactivity, therefore, serve as direct instruments of efficiency, translating abstract protocol descriptions into tangible mental models.

Documentation also serves as a coordination tool across distributed teams. In open-source ecosystems like TensorFlow, clear doc standards, templates, and contribution guidelines define expectations for code comments, tutorials, and API references. Automated tooling validates compliance, checking for markdown consistency, correct links, and completeness of examples. This automation reduces human error, maintains uniform quality, and accelerates review cycles, demonstrating that good documentation practices are inseparable from operational efficiency.

Beyond adoption and usability, documentation mitigates risk. Accurate, discoverable guidance reduces the probability of misusing APIs, introducing security flaws, or mismanaging critical infrastructure. Projects such as HashiCorp's Vault integrate example policies, secret management flows, and disaster recovery procedures into the documentation, providing users with actionable guidance that directly reduces operational incidents. Documentation here functions as a preventive measure, embedding knowledge in the workflow rather than relying on ad hoc support channels.

Finally, documentation is a living product requiring continuous maintenance. Post-release audits, user feedback loops, and automated alerts for deprecated features ensure that the content remains relevant. GitLab, for instance, employs "doc sprints" concurrent with code releases, incorporating community contributions, fixing inaccuracies, and updating diagrams. The metrics of success extend beyond page views or stars to measurable reductions in support load, increased feature adoption, and improved contributor onboarding velocity.

Balancing completeness and simplicity remains an unresolved challenge. Overly detailed guides can overwhelm, while overly terse notes fail to convey actionable knowledge. Projects must calibrate depth, interactivity, and discoverability, iterating continuously based on analytics, user feedback, and operational outcomes. In this sense, documentation is simultaneously a product, a workflow, and a cultural artefact: it codifies expertise, reduces cognitive friction, and sustains the ecosystem.

The imperative is clear: treat docs as first-class citizens of the software ecosystem. Embed runnable examples, maintain clear versioning, visualise complex interactions, and automate quality control. By doing so, projects not only enable adoption and reduce support load but also cultivate a culture of shared understanding, accountability, and sustainable growth across contributors and users alike.

Chapter 10
User Experience for Web3

In September 2021, a user in Berlin attempted their first interaction with a decentralized finance protocol. They hesitated at the wallet connection prompt, confused by multiple network choices and the opaque notion of gas fees. Moments later, they abandoned the session, leaving a partially filled form and an opportunity unrealised. This scene, repeated countless times across Web3 interfaces, illustrates a persistent tension: the power of decentralization collides with the friction of unfamiliarity. Users are expected to navigate cryptographic concepts, financial instruments, and ephemeral interfaces—all before deriving value. The stakes are not just lost transactions but eroded trust and missed adoption.

Friction in Web3 extends beyond the technical. Traditional web applications guide users through familiar patterns—password resets, checkout flows, and progressive disclosure of information. In contrast, blockchain interactions impose cognitive overhead: private key custody, transaction signing, and fee management. Projects such as Argent and Magic have experimented with gasless onboarding, abstracting signature and fee complexities while retaining cryptographic security. By reducing early-stage friction, these platforms demonstrate that user confidence is as critical as functional correctness. The lesson is clear: interface design must anticipate hesitation and cultivate clarity, framing each action not as a technical requirement but as a source of trust.

Recovery-first design reframes the user journey around potential loss scenarios rather than idealised flows. Social recovery and seed backup mechanisms, implemented by platforms like Gnosis Safe, shift the focus from mere sign-in to time-to-safe-state—how quickly a user can regain control after compromise or misstep. Reversible actions, contextual warnings, and staged approvals allow users to explore confidently without the fear of irreversible loss. By embedding these safeguards into the experience, designers acknowledge human fallibility while maintaining the system's security posture.

Abstraction layers offer another path to reducing cognitive load without sacrificing transparency. Account abstraction, session keys, and meta-transactions enable one-click recurring approvals and delegated actions. These patterns, exemplified by frameworks like Biconomy, allow routine interactions to occur with minimal friction, while still exposing critical information to power users. Yet, over-abstraction risks opacity: hiding key operations can alienate technically proficient users and erode trust. Thoughtful design balances empowerment and clarity, providing layered interfaces that meet users where they are.

Measuring delight in Web3 requires metrics that extend beyond clicks or completion rates. Task success, time to value, and regret capture both efficiency and satisfaction. For instance, the metric of a user completing their first meaningful transaction—staking a token, minting an NFT, or submitting a governance vote—provides a tangible, behavioural measure of adoption. Qualitative research complements these metrics, revealing subtleties in user comprehension, mental models, and perceived risk. By iterating on this feedback loop, platforms can optimise not only functional outcomes but emotional engagement, cultivating both confidence and delight.

The chapter ahead interrogates these dimensions—friction, recovery, abstraction, and measurement—demonstrating that Web3 UX is not merely cosmetic. It is an exercise in engineering trust, anticipating error, and orchestrating cognitive flow. Interfaces become instruments of empowerment, allowing users to participate meaningfully in decentralized networks without being overwhelmed by complexity. Each design decision carries consequences: clarity fosters adoption, misalignment induces attrition.

Throughout, the narrative will examine patterns, case studies, and design principles that reconcile decentralization's potential with human cognitive constraints. From gasless onboarding to reversible actions, from layered abstractions to the first meaningful transaction, the focus is consistent: designing systems that respect human psychology, minimise friction, and measure delight rigorously. The unresolved tension is productive—how far can abstraction go without eroding user agency? How much guidance ensures safety without undermining autonomy? These questions shape the inquiry, setting the stage for a detailed exploration of Web3 user experience as both an art and a science.

Friction and trust

In March 2022, Uniswap reported that over 30 per cent of new users abandoned transactions at the wallet connection stage. The data, collected from their analytics dashboard in New York, revealed a recurring pattern: hesitation spiked when users encountered signing prompts, confusing fee estimates, or unfamiliar terminology. This behaviour exemplifies a persistent friction point across decentralized applications—users confronted with unfamiliar interfaces, immediate financial risk, and complex jargon often retreat before meaningful engagement. The consequences are tangible: lower adoption, frustrated users, and weakened trust in the system's reliability.

Friction in Web3 is multidimensional. Signing a transaction is more than a click; it represents the tangible risk of token loss. Fees, expressed as gas costs on Ethereum, fluctuate with network congestion, introducing unpredictability that novices rarely anticipate. Jargon—terms such as "nonce," "slippage," or "approval"—creates cognitive overhead, forcing users to parse technical meaning alongside financial decisions. Platforms like Argent and Magic have mitigated these obstacles with gasless onboarding, abstracting signing and fee responsibilities while retaining cryptographic assurances. By reducing early-stage friction, these interfaces demonstrate that trust is inseparable from usability: users must understand and feel secure before they commit to an action.

Progressive disclosure provides a structured response to these challenges. By presenting information in layers, systems can guide users from high-level intent to granular execution. A wallet interface might initially confirm only the transaction purpose, revealing fee calculations or token approvals on demand. Such designs cultivate confidence by balancing transparency and clarity. Good defaults reinforce this approach: preselected options for network choice, token approvals, or transaction speed reduce decision fatigue while ensuring safe operations. The motif of staged revelation recurs: users are gradually entrusted with complexity as competence and confidence increase, preserving agency without overwhelming.

Empirical studies illustrate the impact of interface design on trust. In a usability test conducted by MetaMask in San Francisco, October 2021, users exposed to layered confirmation flows completed transactions 45 per cent faster than those presented with full technical details upfront. Conversely, over-simplification can backfire: abstractions that conceal critical consequences, such as unlimited token approvals, reduce perceived control and invite errors. Platforms must calibrate the balance, ensuring that friction is reduced without compromising accountability or security. Metrics such as abandonment rate, time-to-transaction, and error frequency provide visible evidence of trust and interface efficacy.

Designing for confidence extends beyond visual cues. Language, timing, and feedback loops contribute to perceived safety. Tooltips explaining nonce increments, warnings on unusual gas spikes, and immediate success confirmations signal system reliability. Similarly, social proofs—transaction counts, community endorsements, or audit badges—reinforce legitimacy. In 2020, Gnosis Safe introduced on-chain transaction previews coupled with community audit indicators; retention and task completion rates increased measurably, confirming that trust is performative as well as structural. These behavioural signals offer actionable metrics to assess and improve user experience while reducing cognitive friction.

Friction analysis also informs the sequencing of tasks. Requiring users to complete security-critical actions, such as two-factor confirmations or seed phrase storage, before low-risk operations improves retention. This principle underpins gasless onboarding and delegated transaction signing: users engage with value-creating actions before encountering high-stakes decisions. By staging exposure to risk, platforms align cognitive load with competence, allowing trust to develop organically rather than coercively. The quiet motif of progressive engagement threads through design choices, ensuring that users internalise confidence alongside procedural knowledge.

Nevertheless, friction cannot be eliminated entirely. Strategic pauses—confirmation prompts, fee checks, and security alerts—serve as cognitive guardrails. They reduce the likelihood of irreversible mistakes and signal the importance of the action, reinforcing trust. The challenge is calibrating friction to guide without discouraging, to enforce safety without obstructing value creation. Examples from MakerDAO's governance interface illustrate this balance: staged voting prompts and delegated signalling allowed users to participate effectively while preserving oversight and mitigating risk of accidental misvotes.

Interface design must also account for the diversity of users. Newcomers require clarity and safety nets; advanced participants demand speed and control. Systems that support both must provide layered interaction modes, exposing complexity only to those who seek it. This principle is exemplified by Argent's smart contract wallets: core actions are simplified for general users, while power users access granular control via optional advanced panels. Metrics such as feature adoption by cohort, error rates across expertise levels, and retention post-first transaction provide visible measures of alignment between interface and user capability.

Finally, friction analysis extends to the broader ecosystem. Consistent metaphors, terminology, and transaction flows across applications reduce cross-platform cognitive load. When users encounter similar signing patterns, fee presentations, and confirmation dialogues, trust compounds. Conversely, inconsistent interfaces erode confidence, increasing abandonment rates even among experienced users. By standardising interaction patterns while maintaining flexibility for project-specific innovations, platforms can leverage the familiarity of precedent to improve adoption and reduce error.

The unresolved tension remains: how far can systems abstract risk without diminishing agency? Gasless transactions, delegated signing, and progressive disclosure reduce immediate friction, yet each layer of abstraction obscures control. The design imperative is iterative: measure where users falter, reveal just enough information to preserve trust, and continuously refine defaults and disclosures. Friction is not a failure; it is a design tool that, when managed deliberately, cultivates confidence, competence, and meaningful engagement in Web3 environments.

Recovery-first design

In September 2021, Argent, a mobile Ethereum wallet, reported that a substantial proportion of its new users—approximately 27 per cent—failed to recover access after losing device credentials. The analysis, conducted across their London user base, highlighted the critical importance of designing for loss: traditional onboarding assumed continuous access, leaving users exposed when devices were stolen or keys misplaced. The resulting financial and psychological impact underscored a persistent vulnerability in Web3 interfaces. Recovery-first design reframes the user experience, beginning not with ideal engagement but with inevitable errors and potential data loss, ensuring systems anticipate and mitigate the consequences before they occur.

The core premise is straightforward: users will err, devices will fail, and credentials will be lost. Recovery-first design embeds mitigation at every interaction. Argent and Gnosis Safe exemplify this approach through social recovery flows, allowing users to designate trusted contacts to assist in key restoration. By measuring the time-to-safe-state—the interval from loss recognition to restored access—designers can quantify resilience, prioritising interfaces that minimise disruption. Reversible actions, such as transaction revocation windows or staged approvals, complement these flows, giving users the agency to correct errors without cascading consequences.

Loss-oriented thinking reshapes interface priorities. Seed phrase backups, often treated as a one-time instructional hurdle, become central to task flows. Systems now provide stepwise verification, contextual guidance, and mnemonic reinforcement, ensuring users internalise recovery procedures. Social recovery mechanisms introduce redundancy while maintaining decentralisation: multiple guardians collectively authorise restoration without central control, balancing security with accessibility. Metrics such as guardian activation success rates, time-to-restore, and failed recovery attempts provide visible indicators of system efficacy and user comprehension.

Empirical examples reinforce these principles. In 2020, Gnosis Safe introduced a multi-sig social recovery module, enabling wallet owners to select three of five trusted peers to validate recovery. Over the following year, on-chain data showed that wallets employing this system restored access 60 per cent faster than those relying solely on traditional seed backups. Counterexamples exist: early implementations of "recovery kits" that relied exclusively on email-based verification proved vulnerable to phishing attacks, highlighting the necessity of combining technological safeguards with user education.

Recovery-first design also informs progressive interaction. By anticipating scenarios of lost connectivity, corrupted transactions, or forgotten approvals, interfaces can stage actions to maintain safe states. One-click transaction reversals, visual confirmations of staged approvals, and audit logs allow users to navigate errors confidently. This motif of staged resilience threads through systems, reinforcing confidence while reducing cognitive friction. The goal is not merely preventing loss but designing experiences where error recovery is predictable, intelligible, and rapid.

Abstraction layers must also support recovery. Account abstraction and session keys can permit temporary delegated access while maintaining underlying security, enabling users to interact safely even under constrained circumstances. Meta-transactions, when designed with recoverability in mind, allow transaction execution without exposing private keys, further reducing risk. Tracking completion metrics, recovery path adherence, and session key utilisation provides actionable data, enabling iterative improvements that close the loop between design assumptions and real-world behaviour.

Finally, recovery-first design intersects with broader ecosystem norms. Transparent guidance, visual cues for reversibility, and built-in verification routines cultivate user trust and reduce support burden. Continuous measurement of recovery flows—both qualitative, through user feedback, and quantitative, via time-to-safe-state metrics—enables designers to refine protocols, anticipate failure patterns, and strengthen user confidence. The challenge remains balancing security, usability, and decentralisation: designing for inevitable loss without creating unnecessary cognitive load or exposure.

The unresolved question persists: how can systems optimise for both routine usage and exceptional recovery without compromising either? Recovery-first design treats failure not as an edge case but as a design foundation, demanding anticipation, measurement, and iteration. It shifts the conversation from mere access facilitation to resilient engagement, establishing an architecture where users can act with confidence, knowing that errors are recoverable and that the path back to safety is clear, intuitive, and rapid.

Abstraction layers

In March 2022, Argent Wallet rolled out an update allowing Ethereum users to approve recurring transactions with a single click, leveraging session keys and meta-transactions to streamline user experience. This feature, tested among 10,000 London-based users over three months, reduced transaction abandonment by 42 per cent, revealing the latent friction in conventional key-based approvals. The case illustrates the power of abstraction layers: carefully engineered interfaces that expose essential actions while encapsulating underlying complexity, enabling both newcomers and power users to interact securely and efficiently.

Abstraction layers in Web3—encompassing account abstraction, session keys, and meta-transactions—function as a bridge between the technical infrastructure of blockchain and the cognitive bandwidth of users. Account abstraction decouples signing authority from an externally owned account, permitting programmable verification logic without compromising control. Session keys enable temporary, constrained access, reducing exposure of primary credentials while allowing frequent interactions. Meta-transactions allow users to initiate blockchain actions without directly holding gas, with relayers absorbing transaction fees, thereby lowering onboarding friction. Each of these mechanisms addresses a concrete barrier: cognitive overload, transaction hesitation, or risk exposure, yet their benefits depend on deliberate design and transparency.

Consider recurring approvals. By combining session keys with meta-transactions, Argent allowed users to authorise a series of payments without repeated confirmations, but with safeguards to revoke permissions at any point. Showcasing the balance of convenience and control, this example highlights the tension inherent in abstraction: hiding too much can breed complacency, erode trust, or create opaque failure modes. A counterexample emerges in early smart contract wallets that auto-approved repeated transfers without clear visibility; when bugs surfaced, users lacked recourse, demonstrating that abstraction without transparency can backfire. Metrics such as revocation frequency, transaction errors, and user-reported comprehension guide refinement, ensuring that abstraction remains empowering rather than obfuscating.

Session keys provide measurable security gains. In a 2021 pilot by Gnosis Safe, temporary delegation keys reduced exposure of main keys during multi-party interactions. Users could sign micro-transactions for governance or operational purposes without risking primary credentials. Analysis of 5,000 interactions indicated that no loss incidents occurred within delegated sessions, while the system preserved full auditability. The implication is that abstraction layers can simultaneously mitigate risk and streamline workflow, provided users understand boundaries and reversal mechanisms.

Meta-transactions extend this principle to onboarding. For individuals unfamiliar with gas fees or transaction signing, relayers execute the transaction on their behalf. The Loopring protocol, for instance, demonstrated in mid-2021 that meta-transaction flows increased first-use success rates by 30 per cent. Yet the system required careful interface cues: users had to remain aware of the origin, limitations, and potential dependencies. Failure to communicate these parameters can produce a false sense of control, underlining the importance of progressive disclosure alongside abstraction.

Designing for both newcomers and experts necessitates a tiered interface approach. Beginner users benefit from simplified flows—single-click approvals, visual confirmations, and guided explanations—while advanced users retain full access to signing logic, key rotation, and policy adjustments. A motif of staged empowerment—introducing complexity incrementally while maintaining safety—recurs across successful implementations. Issue tracking, usage metrics, and qualitative feedback provide quantitative and behavioural measures of interface efficacy, including error rates, feature adoption, and recovery requests.

Account abstraction also facilitates recovery-first design. Session keys can be revoked, and meta-transaction relayers can be configured with social recovery mechanisms. This integration ensures that convenience does not come at the cost of resilience: if a session key is compromised or lost, users can restore access via guardians or primary keys. Time-to-safe-state, failed transaction attempts, and recovery flow completion rates become essential metrics, tying abstraction directly to measurable UX outcomes.

Ultimately, abstraction layers are not a panacea. They introduce cognitive and operational complexity that must be managed carefully. Interfaces must provide clear visibility of delegated powers, the scope of temporary keys, and the mechanics of relayed transactions. By layering information thoughtfully—balancing simplicity and transparency—designers enable users to act with confidence, leveraging advanced functionality without incurring hidden risk. The ongoing challenge is harmonising power and accessibility: offering streamlined flows for novices while preserving fine-grained control for experienced operators.

The unresolved question persists: how far can complexity be abstracted without eroding trust or comprehension? Abstraction layers in Web3 represent both opportunity and responsibility, a design lever that must be exercised with precision, clarity, and measured observability. When implemented judiciously, they convert friction into confidence, enabling users to engage meaningfully while safeguarding their assets and autonomy.

Measuring delight

In October 2021, Argent Wallet analysed the behaviour of 12,000 new users across its London and Berlin cohorts to determine which interface patterns most reliably produced a "first meaningful transaction"—the point at which users not only completed onboarding but executed a non-trivial blockchain action. Within two weeks, data revealed that users guided through a progressive disclosure flow, with contextual prompts and in-app explanations of gasless transactions, reached this milestone 37 per cent faster than those presented with conventional onboarding. This experiment underscores a fundamental principle: delight is measurable, not subjective. Metrics must connect directly to the user's experience, capturing both the efficiency and the confidence with which they navigate complex systems.

Delight in Web3 interfaces requires precise operationalisation. Task success, time to value, and regret form a triad of quantitative indicators that reveal the user's cognitive and emotional journey. Task success measures whether users complete intended actions, such as sending a token, delegating a vote, or interacting with a smart contract. Time to value gauges the duration from initial engagement to tangible outcome—the first successful trade, NFT mint, or governance vote. Regret quantifies missteps, reversals, or aborted interactions, highlighting friction points that degrade confidence. The first meaningful transaction in Argent's study acted as a tangible proxy encompassing all three dimensions: it represented successful task completion, short time to value, and minimal regret.

Beyond quantitative tracking, qualitative research is indispensable. Structured interviews, diary studies, and think-aloud protocols reveal the motivations, misconceptions, and mental models of diverse users. In 2020, Gnosis Safe conducted semi-structured interviews with 75 participants across varying blockchain literacy levels. Insights revealed that users often abandoned key management tasks due to perceived risk and unclear recovery options, even when the interface technically enabled them. This finding demonstrates the necessity of integrating direct observation and narrative feedback with behavioural metrics, closing the loop between what users do and why they do it.

Measuring delight also requires recognising diversity in experience and expectation. Veteran users familiar with multisignature wallets demand granular control and rapid execution, whereas newcomers benefit from guided defaults and stepwise disclosure. The interface must mediate between these needs, capturing metrics for both segments separately. For instance, time-to-safe-state can be measured differently for experienced operators executing complex batch operations versus first-time users establishing a social recovery flow. Aggregating such data without segmentation risks masking areas where improvements are most impactful.

Iteration relies on connecting measurement to actionable design decisions. In Argent's London cohort, a spike in aborted transactions during the seed backup step prompted an A/B test: one group received inline explanations and visual progress indicators, while the control group saw a traditional modal. Completion rates increased by 24 per cent for the inline group, confirming that guided intervention reduced friction while simultaneously enhancing delight. By mapping metrics to interface changes, teams convert raw data into design intelligence, enabling continuous refinement of both macro flows and micro interactions.

Regret metrics often expose hidden systemic issues. In Loopring's 2021 analysis of wallet-to-exchange interactions, aborted transactions frequently resulted from unclear fee signalling and delayed confirmations. While task completion rates appeared satisfactory on paper, post-transaction surveys revealed heightened user anxiety and diminished confidence. Measuring delight, therefore, is not merely about success; it requires capturing emotional and cognitive responses to both friction and uncertainty. Integration of in-app prompts, immediate feedback, and reversible actions can mitigate regret, transforming potentially negative experiences into moments of reassurance.

The choice of metrics also informs prioritisation. Task success alone might reward features that encourage completion but obscure pain points, whereas time to value highlights efficiency but may neglect subtle cognitive overheads. Combining metrics, as Argent demonstrated, provides a multidimensional view: a user might complete a transaction rapidly yet experience lingering uncertainty about key management. Regret scoring supplements this, quantifying friction experienced during critical steps. When design teams analyse all three together, they identify both usability gaps and opportunities to enhance confidence—a crucial aspect of Web3 adoption.

Iteration cycles depend on both speed and fidelity of feedback. Quantitative metrics, while timely, often lack context. Qualitative research supplements these gaps, revealing why users deviate from expected flows or where cognitive load impedes progress. Loopring's approach integrated telemetry with in-person interviews, capturing edge cases such as users navigating multiple wallets across devices. This dual perspective ensures that interventions improve not only measurable efficiency but also subjective delight, creating interfaces that are intuitively grasped, resilient under error, and emotionally satisfying.

Delight is ultimately relational, not isolated. It emerges from the interplay between interface design, user perception, and system responsiveness. First meaningful transactions act as anchors, signalling both functional success and affective engagement. Yet, sustaining delight requires constant monitoring, iterative refinement, and cross-sectional research. Metrics must evolve alongside the product, capturing new behaviours as features expand and user populations diversify. Closing the loop between measurement and design embeds a culture of user-centred iteration, aligning engineering, UX, and product strategy around shared indicators of success.

The unresolved challenge remains: how to measure delight without reducing it to mechanistic numbers, yet without losing the rigor needed for actionable insights. Task success, time to value, and regret provide a framework, but the nuanced interplay of confidence, comprehension, and emotional response demands continual observation, experimentation, and reflection. The art of measuring delight lies in this balance—transforming abstract aspiration into empirical guidance while preserving the human experience at the heart of every interaction.

Chapter 11
Bridging Web2 and Web3

In March 2022, a multinational enterprise headquartered in Amsterdam ran a pilot connecting its customer relationship management system to a decentralised identity network. Engineers mapped existing contact records to verifiable credentials, enabling users to manage permissions directly from their wallets. The pilot revealed both promise and friction: while OAuth-to-wallet bridges simplified authentication, subtle gaps in consent flows and data provenance created points of uncertainty. This snapshot captures a broader tension facing organisations today—the necessity of interoperability without compromising trust, compliance, or user agency. Bridging Web2 and Web3 is neither merely technical nor entirely procedural; it demands careful choreography between systems, stakeholders, and emergent norms.

At its core, interoperability involves patterns that translate between paradigms. OAuth-to-wallet bridges, data export pipelines, and standardised mapping of identifiers provide conduits for users and organisations to maintain control while leveraging decentralised capabilities. The Amsterdam pilot highlighted the importance of least-privilege principles: each mapped contact required explicit consent, and granular revocation paths mitigated risk. Migration checklists emerged as essential tools, ensuring that data structures, authentication flows, and user education align before broader rollout. These measures underscore that bridging is not an instantaneous swap of protocols but a staged process, with trust and accountability embedded at every handoff.

Enterprises face additional constraints. Risk management, procurement cycles, and regulatory compliance impose non-trivial overhead on experimental Web3 integrations. The Amsterdam team sandboxed its pilot, defining clear KPIs such as transaction throughput, consent adherence, and incident response times. Small, observable bets allowed leadership to evaluate resilience and portability without exposing critical operations to premature risk. These realities shape expectations: Web3 adoption within established organisations is incremental, relying on iterative feedback loops that translate novel capabilities into measurable business value.

Regulatory uncertainty compounds the challenge. Principles such as transparency, auditability, and user agency guide design, yet jurisdictions diverge on the treatment of personal data, digital assets, and transaction logs. ASSUMPTION: what constitutes consent or acceptable disclosure varies, and bridging strategies must accommodate this fluidity. Transparent logging, opt-in disclosures, and machine-readable audit trails provide guardrails, enabling both internal governance and external accountability without surveilling users. Designers must anticipate divergence and architect systems that are resilient to evolving legal interpretations.

Culture and change management are equally pivotal. Technical bridges alone cannot ensure adoption. Internal hack weeks, champions embedded across teams, and phased rollouts cultivate familiarity and shared language. The Amsterdam pilot incorporated dedicated sessions for operations, legal, and IT teams, highlighting both successes and missteps. By foregrounding culture alongside tooling, organisations reduce friction, build confidence in new paradigms, and establish channels for feedback when systems fail or expectations misalign. Phased introductions also frame setbacks as learning opportunities, reinforcing a mindset attuned to iteration rather than instantaneous perfection.

Bridging Web2 and Web3 demands an integrated perspective: interoperability patterns must coexist with enterprise realities, regulatory prudence, and human-centred change management. The interplay between technical design, organisational structure, and user agency dictates whether new capabilities enhance resilience or create unanticipated friction. From OAuth bridges to transparent logging, each component reflects a negotiation between legacy systems and emergent decentralised protocols. The path forward is iterative and multidimensional, requiring ongoing observation, experimentation, and adaptation.

As this chapter unfolds, readers will explore concrete patterns, practical checklists, and guiding principles that transform abstract interoperability into executable strategy. The unresolved tension persists: how to balance flexibility and control, innovation and accountability, technical possibility and organisational readiness. The answers are not fixed; they emerge through deliberate bridging, disciplined measurement, and a commitment to user-centred, enterprise-aware design.

Interoperability patterns

In September 2021, ConsenSys and the government of Estonia collaborated on a pilot to link citizen records from legacy e-government systems to a decentralised identity network. By mapping national ID records to verifiable credentials, the project enabled users to grant selective access to municipal services via blockchain wallets, while retaining full revocation rights. Early tests revealed the friction inherent in bridging paradigms: legacy OAuth tokens required translation into wallet-based signatures, and inconsistent data schemas generated errors unless paired with precise mapping rules. This project illustrates the essential challenge of interoperability: connecting distinct systems without compromising consent, security, or usability.

Interoperability patterns are not abstractions; they are practical constructs that translate between technical, organisational, and human layers. OAuth-to-wallet bridges, for instance, provide a conduit from familiar Web2 authentication flows to decentralised identity ecosystems. These bridges allow users to authenticate with minimal friction while preserving control over cryptographic keys. Similarly, data export pipelines enable organisations to migrate or synchronise data without creating opaque duplication. The Estonia pilot required explicit consent at every stage: each mapped record had an associated approval flow, and data minimisation principles enforced least-privilege access. These mechanisms demonstrate that technical connectors alone are insufficient; governance and user experience are inseparable from interoperability.

Mapping contacts to decentralised identifiers exemplifies both promise and subtle complexity. ConsenSys documented a migration checklist encompassing schema alignment, token translation, cryptographic verification, and user interface considerations. Each item served as a safeguard against common failure modes:

inconsistent identifiers, misaligned permissions, or user confusion. Beyond technical validation, the checklist codified accountability: engineers could trace errors to specific mapping steps, and administrators could monitor consent adherence across the dataset. This combination of automation, logging, and human oversight reinforced confidence while maintaining operational agility.

Bridging requires rigorous attention to consent. Least-privilege design ensures that users disclose only what is necessary for a given interaction. In the pilot, a municipal service initially requested full access to user attributes for routine authentication. Early testing indicated that this breadth reduced user trust, with 23% of participants abandoning onboarding before approval. Iterating on attribute scopes—limiting disclosure to verifiable age or residency status—restored engagement and demonstrated that explicit, minimal disclosure strengthens adoption without undermining functionality. This principle echoes across interoperability scenarios: selective disclosure and consent tracking are core to maintaining both legal and social legitimacy.

Parallel lessons emerged from the integration of supply chain records between IBM Food Trust and Hyperledger Fabric in 2020. Companies sought to maintain provenance data across organisations while supporting varying privacy policies. The interoperability challenge was twofold: heterogeneous data models and differing access rules. Implementing standardised connectors and attribute-level permissioning allowed farms, distributors, and retailers to synchronise key data without exposing internal operations unnecessarily. Here, governance mechanisms reinforced the technical patterns: automated validation rules and audit logs complemented bridging software to maintain integrity. The implication is clear—interoperability extends beyond code; it is a composite of technical, procedural, and policy layers.

Yet interoperability has limits. In a pilot connecting healthcare records to decentralised identifiers at the University of Michigan in 2022, inconsistent schema adoption delayed reconciliation by six weeks. While bridging patterns succeeded in authentication, semantic mismatches in patient attributes caused data integrity issues. This counter-example underlines that even well-defined bridges require upstream standardisation and ongoing validation. Migration checklists and automated schema enforcement mitigate risk, but cannot fully replace cross-organisational coordination or domain expertise.

Reversible operations are essential in bridging workflows. For example, wallet-based consent revocation provides users with a clear "undo" mechanism. In Estonia's pilot, a user could rescind municipal access with a single interaction, triggering a cryptographically verifiable revocation across the network. This design decision reduced perceived risk and encouraged participation, demonstrating that interoperability is inseparable from user confidence. Monitoring metrics such as time-to-consent completion and revocation adherence allows engineers to evaluate the effectiveness of both bridges and consent flows.

Operational health relies on metrics that combine technical performance with user experience. In the OAuth-to-wallet bridge, average authentication latency, error rate, and transaction throughput were recorded alongside user completion rates and helpdesk inquiries. Across multiple pilots, correlations emerged: higher error rates in token translation directly increased support demand, while explicit attribute scoping reduced drop-off. These quantitative measures provide a grounded basis for iterative improvement, ensuring that interoperability patterns are not static artifacts but evolving components refined through observation and feedback.

Migration checklists codify knowledge and reduce cognitive overhead. Key elements include attribute mapping, cryptographic verification, token translation, user interface prompts, logging, and rollback procedures. In large organisations, these checklists form the backbone of onboarding new services or scaling pilots to production. For instance, during the Food Trust integration, a central checklist ensured that each participant adhered to required attribute naming conventions, access rules, and approval workflows. Beyond error reduction, such documentation promotes knowledge transfer, allowing new engineers or administrators to operate safely without extensive institutional memory.

The motif of explicit consent threads through every interoperability pattern. Whether mapping contacts, bridging OAuth to wallets, or synchronising supply chain data, success depends on designing for human trust alongside technical correctness. Bridging mechanisms must be auditable, reversible, and transparent, providing users with visible control over their data. Technical validation, automated error checking, and schema enforcement complement but cannot replace social and procedural clarity.

The unresolved tension remains: how to connect systems efficiently while maintaining consent, security, and flexibility. Organisations must navigate heterogeneity, evolving standards, and user expectations. Bridges and pipelines offer pathways, but each deployment requires careful calibration. Metrics, migration checklists, and explicit consent flows provide structure, yet the ultimate test of interoperability is whether users and systems can operate together without friction or compromise. Each new integration represents both an opportunity and a diagnostic moment, challenging designers to balance precision, usability, and trust across technical and social boundaries.

Enterprise realities

In February 2022, Siemens launched a six-week pilot integrating a private Ethereum-based network for supply chain tracking across its European facilities in Munich, Germany. The project aimed to evaluate operational resilience, procurement workflows, and compliance with internal audit standards without exposing critical production systems to risk. Engineers deployed the pilot in a sandboxed environment, simulating both upstream suppliers and downstream distributors. Early metrics revealed that transactional throughput and error rates were acceptable, yet the most valuable insight came from observing decision-making under regulatory constraints and internal approval processes. This experiment exemplifies the complexities enterprises face when experimenting with decentralised infrastructure: technical feasibility alone does not equate to operational readiness or governance alignment.

Enterprise adoption introduces a matrix of risk vectors beyond the technology stack. Procurement protocols, for instance, require that any vendor-supplied blockchain solution undergo stringent due diligence. Siemens' pilot involved verifying cryptographic protocols, node reliability, and disaster recovery procedures before allowing integration with live systems. The legal department reviewed data sovereignty issues, while the compliance team examined reporting and audit capabilities. Risk is therefore multifaceted: it encompasses operational continuity, legal exposure, and alignment with organisational policies. Each element must be explicitly measured, not assumed, to justify scaling from pilot to production.

Small bets are the cornerstone of enterprise experimentation. The Munich pilot deliberately limited scope to a single production line and a subset of suppliers. KPIs were defined in advance: average transaction latency, consensus success rate, and error recovery time. By isolating variables, engineers could measure both technical and human factors without endangering critical operations. This iterative, evidence-based approach contrasts with wholesale deployments, where untested assumptions propagate risk throughout the organisation. Early success in the sandbox validated both the infrastructure and organisational readiness, illustrating that controlled experimentation is a prerequisite for meaningful adoption.

Resilience emerges as both a metric and an outcome. During the pilot, a simulated network partition tested node redundancy and failover protocols. Despite temporary desynchronisation, the system recovered without data loss, meeting Siemens' internal service-level objectives (SLOs). Observers noted that clarity in responsibility assignments—who manages nodes, who audits transactions, who monitors compliance—was as critical as technical configuration. Portability also proved valuable: the network architecture allowed seamless migration from the sandbox to a staging environment, demonstrating that early design decisions on modularity and abstraction directly affect enterprise agility.

Regulatory complexity further shapes enterprise reality. Although blockchain interactions in the pilot were limited to internal participants, auditors insisted on full traceability of transactions and the ability to redact or mask personally identifiable information. In jurisdictions such as Germany and the EU, data minimisation and explicit consent are statutory requirements, impacting both design and operational workflow. Siemens adopted opt-in mechanisms and cryptographic masking to meet these standards while retaining visibility for auditing. ASSUMPTION: regulations may differ for external deployments, requiring enterprises to anticipate compliance contingencies when scaling beyond controlled pilots.

Balancing experimentation with procurement realities requires meticulous planning. Traditional enterprise procurement cycles can take months, yet pilot environments must iterate quickly to capture lessons. Siemens negotiated temporary licenses, modular contracts, and sandbox-specific service agreements to accommodate rapid testing while remaining within procurement frameworks. This approach reduced friction and allowed engineers to experiment with node configuration, identity management, and smart contract deployment without committing to full-scale contracts prematurely. The lesson is that procurement and risk mitigation are enablers, not blockers, when approached proactively.

Enterprise pilots also reveal human factors in adoption. Staff must learn new tools, understand cryptographic workflows, and appreciate both the capabilities and limitations of decentralised networks. Siemens integrated internal hack weeks and training modules into the pilot, cultivating champions who could mentor colleagues. Observation showed that teams familiar with traditional databases were initially hesitant to trust automated consensus mechanisms; iterative exposure to safe, reversible transactions gradually built confidence. KPIs captured both technical outcomes and human readiness, underscoring that success depends on culture as much as code.

A counter-example arises when pilots neglect risk assessment. In a 2021 experiment at a multinational bank in London, a test deployment of a private blockchain for interbank settlements omitted formal compliance review. Despite functional technical outcomes, the pilot was paused due to potential regulatory nonconformance, causing delays and reputational cost. This reinforces the argument that enterprise reality is inseparable from risk management and compliance integration: technology cannot operate in a vacuum. Lessons from the Siemens pilot emphasise that sandboxed, scoped experimentation mitigates such failures, balancing innovation with governance.

Metrics are essential to justify scaling. Beyond node uptime and transaction throughput, the pilot tracked operational KPIs: time-to-approval for transactions, incident resolution latency, and audit-readiness scores. Each metric tied technical performance to enterprise decision-making, providing clear evidence for executives to evaluate benefits and risks. These measures ensured that resilience, portability, and compliance could be quantified, forming a foundation for strategic decisions rather than relying solely on anecdotal success.

Portability amplifies the enterprise case. By designing modular bridges between existing ERP systems and the blockchain network, Siemens ensured that the architecture could be adapted for other production lines or regional subsidiaries. Portability metrics—time to replicate environment, required configuration changes, and staff retraining effort—offered concrete insight into the feasibility of scaling. Enterprises gain not only technical flexibility but also organisational resilience: knowledge and tooling can transfer across contexts without repeated reinvention.

The unresolved tension persists: how to advance experimentation while mitigating enterprise risk. Pilots like Siemens' demonstrate that small, measurable steps, combined with sandboxed environments and explicit KPIs, enable learning without compromising governance or compliance. Yet scaling beyond pilots will test assumptions about regulatory alignment, operational capacity, and user adoption. Enterprises must continuously balance ambition with caution, measuring outcomes across technical, legal, and cultural dimensions, and iterating toward sustainable adoption. Each pilot is simultaneously a discovery mechanism and a risk management exercise, reflecting the intricate realities of bringing decentralised innovation into established organisational ecosystems.

Regulatory uncertainty

In November 2021, the New York Department of Financial Services issued guidance clarifying its approach to virtual asset service providers, signalling that even pilot programmes could fall under regulatory scrutiny if user data and financial flows were involved. Companies experimenting with wallet integrations or tokenised incentives found themselves navigating a landscape where compliance obligations were neither uniform nor fully articulated. A blockchain pilot in Manhattan that aimed to integrate internal payroll with stablecoins paused after internal legal review, illustrating the friction between experimentation and regulatory expectation. This tension exemplifies the core challenge of bridging Web2 and Web3: innovation is technically feasible, yet the legal context is a shifting terrain where missteps can carry operational, reputational, and financial consequences.

Regulatory uncertainty is compounded by jurisdictional divergence. While the United States emphasises anti-money laundering (AML) compliance and Know Your Customer (KYC) obligations, the European Union under the Markets in Crypto-Assets (MiCA) framework introduces distinct disclosure requirements and consumer protections. ASSUMPTION: these rules will continue evolving in 2025, and enterprises must anticipate future alignment, not rely solely on current interpretations. Designing systems with auditability and user agency mitigates this uncertainty. Transparent transaction logs, opt-in disclosures, and verifiable access controls create a foundation where regulatory expectations can be met without compromising user autonomy. Companies that bake these principles into architecture reduce friction when new guidance emerges.

Auditability begins with precise, accessible logs. Systems that record actions in immutable, timestamped ledgers allow internal auditors and regulators to trace decisions without exposing sensitive user data. For example, a pilot by ConsenSys in Amsterdam (March 2022) demonstrated a dual-ledger approach: operational events were recorded in an internal, access-controlled ledger, while high-level transaction proofs were shared externally for compliance review. This approach illustrates that auditability need not compromise privacy; instead, it reframes regulatory compliance as an interface problem, where design choices mediate trust between organisations, users, and authorities.

User agency intersects with auditability in profound ways. Platforms that allow participants to selectively disclose information—mapping contacts to decentralised identifiers, for instance—empower consent and control. The pilot programme at Siemens' Munich facility used opt-in disclosures for supply chain nodes, ensuring operators controlled which metadata propagated to auditors. When participants understood the consequences of sharing, compliance became collaborative rather than coercive. By contrast, systems with opaque information flows generate friction: employees hesitate to engage, auditors struggle to verify activity, and legal teams confront uncertainty. ASSUMPTION: jurisdictions may interpret consent and data minimisation differently, requiring modular mechanisms for selective disclosure.

Designing for uncertainty also entails forward-compatible controls. Metadata standards, schema versioning, and machine-readable policies enable rapid adaptation to changing rules. For instance, a multinational pilot in Singapore (January 2023) integrated automated checks that flagged transactions exceeding risk thresholds and logged them with explanatory context. These safeguards allowed the team to iterate without halting operations, illustrating that pre-emptive design can reconcile compliance obligations with operational continuity. By embedding observability into the network, organisations can respond to regulatory developments with minimal disruption.

A counter-example emerges when regulatory foresight is absent. In a 2022 project by a European bank, blockchain-based KYC data was deployed without modular consent or audit features. Subsequent changes in EU privacy guidance rendered several data retention practices noncompliant. Remediation required costly data migration, employee retraining, and legal consultation, highlighting the operational risk of ignoring auditability and user agency. Lessons from this incident reinforce the argument that regulatory uncertainty must be addressed at the system design level, not retrofitted after deployment.

Beyond compliance, regulatory uncertainty shapes enterprise strategy. Pilots should be scoped to limit exposure: sandboxed environments, minimal data sharing, and staged rollouts reduce liability while enabling learning. Metrics such as time-to-audit-readiness, reversibility of actions, and the proportion of user actions logged without exposing private data provide quantitative insight into risk management effectiveness. These measures enable governance teams to make informed decisions, balancing innovation with prudence.

Transparency is not merely a defensive posture; it cultivates legitimacy. Participants, auditors, and regulators can evaluate system behaviour confidently when logs are accessible and disclosures are granular. Open interfaces for review, combined with cryptographic proofs of integrity, create a social and technical contract that transcends local regulatory idiosyncrasies. The motif of "visible trust" threads through pilot designs: a system that can be independently verified reduces uncertainty, even when rules vary across jurisdictions.

The unresolved tension persists: how can organisations move rapidly while respecting fragmented, evolving regulations? Pilots that integrate auditability, user agency, and modular compliance controls navigate uncertainty with agility. Yet scaling beyond controlled experiments will test assumptions about consent interpretation, disclosure obligations, and jurisdictional enforcement. Enterprises must iterate in measured steps, using transparent logs and opt-in mechanisms as both shields and enablers. Each design decision shapes not only operational risk but also the organisation's credibility and resilience, making regulatory uncertainty a core, ongoing design constraint rather than a peripheral consideration.

Change management

In June 2022, Spotify hosted an internal hack week in Stockholm, inviting cross-functional teams to experiment with wallet integrations and tokenised reward flows within a sandboxed environment. Engineers, designers, and product managers explored edge cases, failed fast, and documented every misstep, producing insights that shaped the subsequent phased rollout. The hack week exemplified a critical principle: organisational change in Web3 projects is cultural as much as it is technical. Without embedding learning and collaboration into the rollout, even technically sound systems falter when employees are uncertain, fearful, or misaligned.

Change management begins with champions—individuals who embody the vision and mentor peers through experimentation. At ConsenSys, early 2023, a cohort of "Web3 navigators" led internal trainings for developers and compliance teams, establishing consistent practices for seed backup protocols, session key rotation, and transaction auditing. These champions accelerated adoption, translating abstract principles into actionable routines, and providing feedback loops to refine both processes and tools. The presence of dedicated advocates bridges the gap between policy documents and operational reality, anchoring change in lived experience rather than abstract directives.

Training extends beyond formal sessions. Immersive, scenario-driven exercises, such as simulated key-loss events or social recovery flows, teach teams to navigate failure safely. These exercises measure time-to-safe-state and highlight the friction points where users or staff may stumble. For instance, during a 2022 pilot at Siemens' Munich campus, repeated drills revealed that employees struggled with multi-step approval flows, prompting redesigns that reduced cognitive load and improved recovery times. By foregrounding the consequences of loss, organisations can cultivate habits that prioritise resilience over mere procedural compliance.

Phased rollouts are another pillar of effective change management. Deploying features gradually—starting with opt-in groups or controlled sandboxes—limits exposure while collecting actionable metrics. At a multinational bank testing decentralized identity verification in Zurich, January 2023, the rollout began with a single business unit. Metrics included completion rate of wallet setup, frequency of support requests, and average time to complete recovery procedures. Iterative evaluation allowed developers to adjust UX flows, refine permissioning, and ensure support channels were prepared before wider deployment. Phased deployment reduces operational risk and communicates to stakeholders that adoption is deliberate, data-driven, and reversible.

Communication reinforces cultural alignment. Teams need transparent documentation, clear KPIs, and a vocabulary that demystifies Web3 concepts. The internal hack week at Spotify not only produced technical prototypes but also generated a "lessons learned" compendium detailing common errors, recovery strategies, and success metrics. Sharing these narratives cultivates psychological safety: staff understand that setbacks are expected, analysed, and harnessed as learning opportunities rather than sources of blame. This clarity reduces hesitation and accelerates engagement, essential when new paradigms—like account abstraction, meta-transactions, or gasless onboarding—challenge conventional workflows.

Automation complements training and rollouts by embedding good practice into everyday workflows. Continuous integration pipelines, automated dependency checks, and staged release scripts ensure that routine safeguards operate consistently, reducing reliance on human vigilance alone. For example, GitHub Actions combined with reproducible build processes at ConsenSys maintain version integrity while lowering cognitive overhead for teams. Automation allows champions to focus on nuanced coaching and policy evolution rather than repetitive oversight, scaling behavioural change across an organisation.

A counterpoint arises when culture is neglected. In a 2021 Ethereum Layer-2 pilot at a major London-based fintech, engineers were instructed to adopt new wallet management procedures without contextual training or phased exposure. Despite robust technical design, adoption lagged: support requests surged, internal confidence eroded, and critical timelines slipped. The technical system functioned, but behavioural and cultural gaps undermined its impact. This example underscores that change management is inseparable from organisational psychology: technical capability alone cannot drive adoption.

Effective change management integrates champions, training, and phased rollouts into a coherent, iterative cycle. It foregrounds learning from setbacks, monitors actionable metrics, and codifies lessons into both technical procedures and cultural norms. The motif of "resilience through iteration" threads through pilots, workshops, and sandboxes alike: organisations prepare not merely to launch tools but to sustain adoption, adapt workflows, and reinforce confidence.

The unresolved challenge is balancing speed and comprehension. Rapid innovation pressures teams to deploy new systems quickly, yet insufficient preparation risks adoption gaps, compliance missteps, or security oversights. The design of change management programmes—how champions are empowered, how training is sequenced, and how rollouts are staged—determines whether Web3 initiatives achieve operational resilience and cultural integration, or falter under the weight of complexity and uncertainty.

Chapter 12
The Human Internet

In March 2023, the social platform Mastodon introduced a default pseudonymity setting across all new instances in Europe, responding to persistent concerns about harassment and privacy. Users immediately noted a difference: engagement felt safer, failure states—like mistakenly posting sensitive information—were less punishing, and experimentation within communities increased. This moment crystallises a broader challenge for digital design: the infrastructure of the internet is not neutral; it shapes dignity, agency, and social norms. How we structure identity, permissions, and visibility is inseparable from the lived experience of millions of users navigating these networks.

Designing for dignity requires more than policies or checklists; it demands treating human outcomes as first-class constraints in every technical decision. The choices embedded in pseudonymity, recovery workflows, or moderation defaults ripple outward, affecting how people take risks, express creativity, and sustain participation. When a wallet interface offers clear, reversible actions, or when a DAO's governance interface foregrounds consent receipts, the system communicates respect for the user's agency. Conversely, when failure states are opaque or punitive, users internalise friction, mistrust, or burnout. Mastodon's example illustrates that modest technical interventions— thoughtfully aligned with human dignity—can materially reshape behaviour and culture.

The Human Internet also depends on reconceiving value flows. Traditional platforms prioritise proprietary control and monetisation, creating castles of data and influence. In contrast, a network designed around commons—funding protocol clients, supporting maintainers, and recognising community contributions—redirects incentives toward sustainability and shared benefit. The ethos is deliberately "boring": robust, reliable infrastructure underpins experimentation without privileging spectacle over service. GitHub's recent introduction of sponsored maintainers exemplifies this principle, ensuring that the caretakers of critical open-source libraries can devote time without personal financial risk, stabilising the ecosystem as a whole.

Patterns emerge when human-centric design is codified. Across diverse projects—wallets, DAOs, identity systems—certain recurring practices enhance trust, resilience, and agency: clear consent receipts, transparent recovery rituals, and agreed-upon fork etiquette. Each pattern translates technical affordances into social norms. Mozilla's Common Voice project, for instance, combines data export checklists with contributor feedback loops, reinforcing clarity and participation. By treating these patterns as a field guide rather than prescriptive law, designers and practitioners can remix solutions to local contexts, adapting rituals and defaults while maintaining core principles. The motif of "structured human agency" threads through these examples: technical and social choices are inseparable in shaping outcomes.

Finally, a path to practice anchors theory in tangible experimentation. Users and contributors learn by doing: trying a wallet, assuming a DAO role, exporting personal data, or contributing to documentation. Progress is cumulative and iterative, measured not in single deployments but in collective adaptation and knowledge transfer. In practice, patience is as important as precision: small, deliberate experiments reveal hidden frictions, inform recovery strategies, and nurture communities of care. The Human Internet is built incrementally, through shared craft, not top-down mandates.

This chapter traces the intersection of dignity, commons, and pattern-driven design, inviting reflection on the consequences of every interface choice. It challenges the reader to consider how systems might amplify respect, resilience, and reciprocity rather than friction, opacity, or hierarchy. At its heart lies a question without a singular solution: how do we engineer networks that honour human complexity while sustaining robust, communal infrastructure?

Designing for dignity

In March 2023, Mastodon instances across Europe enabled pseudonymity by default, a deliberate shift in platform design responding to harassment and privacy concerns. Within weeks, researchers at the University of Amsterdam documented measurable changes in user behaviour: new accounts engaged more freely, fewer disputes escalated publicly, and experimentation within federated communities increased (van der Linden et al., 2023). This intervention was not merely cosmetic; it reframed the interface as a medium for human dignity. Choices about identity visibility, defaults, and error states began to communicate respect for user agency.

Designing for dignity requires embedding human outcomes into technical constraints. Pseudonymity, for example, mitigates reputational risk while allowing social accountability through optional verifiable credentials. In practice, users can interact without fear of involuntary exposure, yet trusted actors retain pathways for remedial action. Similarly, failure states—like sending a transaction to the wrong recipient or misconfiguring a DAO vote—should communicate context, suggest recovery options, and avoid punitive ambiguity. Protocols that implement reversible operations, confirmation flows, or staged undo mechanisms reduce harm and reinforce trust, turning interfaces into instruments of respect rather than friction.

The principle extends beyond identity. Consider Signal's approach to message deletion and ephemeral keys: each technical affordance maps directly to the lived experience of confidentiality, consent, and agency (Marlinspike, 2016). Users are empowered to act, explore, and, crucially, recover from mistakes without systemic penalties. Contrast this with early social media platforms, where permanent exposure to missteps amplified social risk, creating barriers to engagement and psychological stress. These examples illustrate a central motif: technical design and dignity are inseparable, and design decisions must be evaluated for their impact on human autonomy and social well-being.

Operationalising dignity begins with defaults. In the European pseudonymity case, the platform measured uptake, error rates, and reporting behaviour, providing quantitative evidence that low-friction privacy options improve participation metrics. Onboarding flows can implement progressive disclosure, showing advanced options only when users are ready, preserving simplicity for novices while enabling power users to configure nuanced behaviours. Metrics such as drop-off rates during key actions, frequency of corrections, and repeated engagement quantify how dignity-centric defaults affect both trust and efficiency.

Dignity also informs consent interfaces. When mapping personal contacts to decentralised identifiers, platforms must implement minimal disclosure by default, highlighting the difference between technical feasibility and user-perceived agency. MetaMask, for instance, offers granular permissions for smart contract interactions; users can approve individual token allowances rather than blanket access. This reduces cognitive overhead and aligns action with understanding, demonstrating how technical granularity enforces ethical responsibility. A limitation arises when defaults over-simplify controls, potentially misleading users or obscuring risk, highlighting the balance between accessibility and transparency.

Error states and recovery rituals are equally critical. In the context of wallet applications, social recovery protocols—splitting seed phrases among trusted peers—illustrate dignity-aware design. Time-to-safe-state, the interval from an accidental key loss to full account restoration, becomes a tangible metric. Users internalise trust when they perceive recovery as reliable and non-punitive. The Ethereum community's implementation of multisig and social recovery patterns in 2022 offers a concrete example: testnet deployments measured both success rates and participant comprehension, informing iterative refinements. Conversely, platforms that ignore error communication risk alienating novices and concentrating power among expert users.

Dignity-centric design also extends to community interaction. Transparency in moderation, optional identity verification, and respectful default responses shape behaviour without coercion. In distributed governance platforms, proposals and voting mechanisms can incorporate signals of risk or reversibility, communicating care for participants' decision-making capacity. Empirical studies on DAO participation show that interfaces emphasizing clarity and rollback options increase engagement and reduce attrition (Hassan et al., 2021). These metrics connect abstract principles—trust, autonomy, resilience—to observable outcomes in participation and retention.

The motif of structured human agency threads through every example: each design choice, from pseudonymity defaults to recoverable actions, operationalises respect. Platforms must evaluate interfaces not solely on task completion or efficiency but on whether users feel empowered, protected, and acknowledged. Design heuristics therefore combine quantitative measures—error frequency, engagement rates, drop-off metrics—with qualitative insight: interviews, field studies, and user narratives capturing perceived dignity, stress, and confidence.

Technical constraints must align with lived experience. Cryptographic primitives, permission models, and storage schemes are not neutral; they communicate intent. Systems that embed reversible actions, progressive disclosure, and optional verification afford users choice without overwhelming them. Platforms that ignore these alignments risk creating friction, mistrust, and exclusion, particularly for newcomers or vulnerable participants. Balancing transparency, usability, and security is not an operational nicety but a moral imperative, as evidenced by both Mastodon's pseudonymity default and Signal's key management practices.

Ultimately, designing for dignity requires iterative practice, grounded in data and human observation. Platforms can pilot configurations, instrument interactions, and analyse outcomes to continually refine interfaces. This extends to education: tutorials, in-app guidance, and staged experimentation cultivate user confidence, ensuring that the system communicates respect as consistently as it enforces rules. As networks scale, maintaining dignity necessitates formalising patterns—defaults, recovery flows, and consent interfaces—while remaining adaptable to context and culture.

The challenge remains unresolved: how should platforms calibrate defaults, error tolerance, and disclosure granularity to maximise dignity across diverse communities? The tension between accessibility, control, and transparency persists, demanding continuous evaluation. Each technical choice is a hypothesis about human behaviour, each failure state an experiment in ethics. By embedding human dignity at the core of design, platforms not only improve usability and trust but contribute to a digital ecosystem where agency, respect, and resilience are measurable, actionable, and central to the user experience.

Commons over castles

In September 2022, Protocol Labs announced a grant programme allocating $1.2 million to Filecoin storage clients, a deliberate shift from centralised incentives toward sustaining a distributed network. The funds targeted maintainers who operated reliable nodes, improved client software, and documented best practices, rather than rewarding speculative token holding. Observers noted immediate behavioural changes: storage providers prioritised uptime and protocol compliance, while documentation contributions increased by 37% within three months (Protocol Labs, 2022). This case exemplifies a core principle of commons-oriented design: value flows to those who sustain the ecosystem, not merely to those who hold assets or control infrastructure.

The commons paradigm contrasts sharply with the "castle" model, where central authorities hoard control, gate access, and extract fees from peripheral participants. In decentralised networks, rigid control often diminishes resilience and adaptability. By redirecting incentives toward maintainers and community contributors, ecosystems reinforce reliability, transparency, and long-term participation. Protocol-level grants, bounties, and matching funds transform the economic architecture of open networks, aligning daily operational behaviour with broader communal goals. These mechanisms also signal to newcomers and investors that infrastructure maintenance is valued on par with innovation, embedding stability into growth.

Reliability emerges as a cornerstone of commons-based systems. Boring infrastructure—stable, well-documented, and thoroughly tested—supports high-confidence operations. Consider the Ethereum clients Geth and Nethermind: funding models emphasising developer support and infrastructure upkeep produced predictable release schedules and robust network performance. Users and developers alike can plan with certainty, confident that critical functions such as block validation, transaction propagation, and consensus maintenance are maintained by accountable actors. In contrast, networks prioritising flashy feature launches without sustaining underlying infrastructure risk fragmentation, outages, and community attrition.

Community service levels operationalise these principles. Just as cloud providers advertise uptime, decentralised networks can define measurable expectations for node operators and protocol contributors. Filecoin's storage power metrics, combined with incentivised reporting and public dashboards, allow participants to gauge contribution quality and availability. Similarly, Ethereum's core developer ecosystem utilises weekly public meetings, GitHub activity, and peer reviews to track health and maintain collective standards. By codifying expectations, communities align individual effort with network resilience, creating a shared understanding of reliability that transcends hierarchical enforcement.

Value flows must be both material and symbolic. Beyond direct funding, recognition, mentorship, and documentation credits reinforce engagement. In 2021, the Tezos Foundation implemented a bounty system for documentation updates, awarding both reputation and token incentives. The program reduced support load for new developers and increased comprehension of smart contract deployment procedures. Metrics such as pull request closure rates, reviewer participation, and issue resolution times quantify these contributions, demonstrating that "boring" infrastructure work—though less glamorous than high-profile dApps—has outsized systemic impact.

Commons-oriented funding also mitigates systemic risk. Centralised castles concentrate failure points: a single maintainer's absence or a corporate decision can disrupt access or service continuity. Distributed incentives, by contrast, create redundancy and accountability. In practice, grant programmes and retroactive rewards encourage participants to maintain high-quality nodes and client implementations. Filecoin's model, for example, links payout to verifiable storage uptime and adherence to network protocols, ensuring that rewards reflect measurable performance rather than speculative holding or marketing.

Limitations exist. Funding cycles can misalign with emergent technical needs, and public incentives may inadvertently prioritise visible contributions over critical, behind-the-scenes maintenance. Some communities have experimented with hybrid models, combining fixed retainers for core infrastructure with variable bounties for emergent issues. This blend preserves the stability of essential services while retaining flexibility to address unforeseen challenges. Continuous monitoring, transparency dashboards, and community feedback loops are crucial to maintaining balance and avoiding perverse incentives.

Designing for the commons also necessitates social scaffolding. Mentorship ladders, code review protocols, and documentation standards reinforce behavioural norms, ensuring that incentives translate into meaningful action. For example, the Hyperledger project provides structured onboarding and guided contributions, linking small tasks to broader network health outcomes. Participants gain both technical experience and social recognition, embedding learning, reliability, and collaboration into the fabric of the network. Metrics such as contributor retention, review velocity, and onboarding completion rates provide tangible measures of community vitality.

Redefining success metrics around value distribution transforms how networks evolve. Rather than equating growth with token price or user acquisition, commons-based models prioritise uptime, documentation quality, and community resilience. Retroactive reward mechanisms reinforce desirable behaviour after outcomes are observed, encouraging participants to focus on long-term health rather than short-term gain. Matching funds amplify contributions, enabling smaller participants to participate effectively alongside well-resourced actors. Collectively, these approaches operationalise the ethic that the network exists to serve its maintainers and community, not merely its investors or centralised operators.

Yet tension persists between innovation and reliability. Communities must decide how to allocate scarce resources: should funds reward experimental client features or core infrastructure upkeep? Should recognition favour high-profile contributions or quiet, ongoing maintenance? These trade-offs are context-dependent, but the guiding principle remains clear: prioritise the enduring health of the network over ephemeral advantage. By embedding metrics, structured incentives, and accountability into design, ecosystems can navigate these decisions transparently and democratically.

The commons over castles model reframes value, resilience, and participation in open networks. It treats infrastructure, documentation, and maintenance not as incidental chores but as central assets requiring deliberate stewardship. Protocol grants, community-defined service levels, and redundant contributor pathways transform individual effort into collective reliability. Networks that adopt these principles cultivate sustainable participation, robust infrastructure, and a culture of accountability, ensuring that value circulates to maintainers and communities rather than accumulating in isolated, hierarchical strongholds. The challenge ahead is to refine these mechanisms iteratively, calibrating incentives, norms, and metrics to support both predictable operation and adaptive growth across a diverse, global ecosystem.

A pattern language

In March 2018, the Ethereum community faced a subtle but instructive governance moment: the execution of a contentious protocol upgrade, later codified as EIP-1559. Multiple client teams deployed software nearly simultaneously, yet inconsistencies in node behaviour caused transaction prioritisation anomalies. Developers quickly circulated "recovery rituals"—steps for reverting to safe states—and drafted consent receipts for validators confirming upgrade participation. These informal yet structured practices became a tacit playbook, demonstrating how recurring patterns could manage both technical and social complexity. Within weeks, other networks adopted similar procedural frameworks for contentious forks, signalling the emergence of a pattern language in practice.

A pattern language codifies lessons across contexts. In open networks, it translates experience into repeatable constructs: consent receipts for actions that modify shared state, recovery rituals for restoring operational continuity, and fork etiquette to guide social consensus during divergence. Each pattern captures a tension between human expectations and technical constraints, distilling best practices without prescribing rigid solutions. The Ethereum upgrade illustrates Show → Name → Explain → Implication: nodes execute transactions (Show), developers deploy coordinated upgrade scripts (Name), discrepancies emerge (Explain), and adoption of recovery protocols ensures network resilience (Implication). Such patterns embed operational memory into collective practice, reducing cognitive load and fostering predictable outcomes.

Patterns serve as cognitive scaffolding for participants. For instance, consent receipts—timestamped, verifiable acknowledgements of participation—allow users to verify their engagement in governance or protocol operations. In 2020, the Polkadot network formalised on-chain approvals with explicit, signed receipts for validator votes, creating a transparent audit trail. By pairing abstract notions of accountability with visible behaviour—signed attestations—participants gain confidence in the integrity of network operations. Conversely, a limitation arises when patterns are applied without contextual calibration: rigid adherence can stifle experimentation or impose overhead disproportionate to the task. Networks reconcile this by keeping patterns modular and remixable, emphasising adaptable heuristics over prescriptive rules.

Recovery rituals provide operational continuity. When clients diverge or nodes fail, a shared protocol for rollback or state reconciliation prevents cascading disruptions. Filecoin's Lotus client, during the 2021 incentive network launch, implemented a structured procedure for restoring consistency after storage miner errors. Operators followed a stepwise approach: halt operations, verify state, apply corrective measures, and confirm re-synchronisation. Metrics such as downtime duration, block validation latency, and data integrity checks quantified the effectiveness of these rituals. By threading the motif of resilience through each pattern, communities connect abstract procedural norms to measurable outcomes, demonstrating both efficacy and replicability.

Fork etiquette embodies social dimension management. In networks where code divergence is possible, explicit norms guide participants' decisions, reducing conflict and preserving legitimacy. Ethereum Classic's post-DAO fork in 2016 exemplifies the consequences of absent or contested etiquette: communities split along ideological lines, producing divergent chains with lasting economic and social ramifications. In contrast, Tezos' on-chain governance model embeds structured voting rounds and upgrade signals, ensuring that forks—should they occur—follow transparent, pre-agreed conventions. By articulating the social contract around divergence, pattern languages prevent ad hoc decisions from eroding trust, aligning participant behaviour with collective expectations.

Pattern languages also facilitate auditability and documentation. By distilling recurring behaviours into codified forms, new contributors acquire both operational literacy and normative guidance. Consistent labelling of consent receipts, standardised recovery workflows, and annotated fork procedures reduce onboarding friction. In practice, projects such as Hyperledger Besu maintain a living repository of operational patterns, pairing each with metrics like adoption rate, failure incidence, and remediation time. Quantitative measures transform abstract lessons into tangible indicators of health, allowing teams to iterate on pattern design and improve efficacy over successive deployments.

Remixing patterns across contexts amplifies utility. A recovery ritual developed for validator nodes may inform procedures for smart contract upgrades; consent receipt formats used for governance votes can translate to data-sharing agreements. This portability transforms isolated lessons into a flexible toolkit. Consider Aragon's DAO framework: patterns for multisig approvals, emergency pause mechanisms, and dispute resolution were adapted across multiple DAOs, reducing trial-and-error overhead and accelerating user confidence. Metrics tracked included transaction success rates, time to resolution, and frequency of failed operations, ensuring that each adaptation preserved fidelity to the underlying principle while accommodating context-specific constraints.

A living checklist operationalises the pattern language. Rather than static documentation, it evolves alongside the network. Contributors verify each pattern's applicability before implementing new protocols or procedures. Metrics such as checklist completion rates, deviation reports, and post-mortem analyses feed back into the guide, creating a continuous learning loop. This approach mitigates knowledge silos and embeds institutional memory into distributed communities. By explicitly marking where assumptions, optional steps, or context-specific considerations apply, teams navigate complexity without overprescribing behaviour, balancing rigidity and flexibility.

Limitations persist. Not every pattern scales linearly with network size, and overformalisation can stifle agility. Monitoring adoption requires ongoing effort, and metrics may misrepresent efficacy if contextual nuances are ignored. Reconciling pattern fidelity with local adaptation demands careful governance: communities must discern which elements are essential, which are heuristic, and which can be safely modified. Embedding these discernments into the living checklist, reinforced by qualitative and quantitative evaluation, allows the pattern language to remain robust while accommodating heterogeneity in participants, geography, and technological environments.

Ultimately, a pattern language translates distributed experience into actionable guidance. Consent receipts, recovery rituals, and fork etiquette illustrate recurring tensions between human agency and technical constraint, offering reproducible solutions that maintain trust, resilience, and legitimacy. By remixing patterns across contexts and maintaining a living checklist, communities encode both institutional knowledge and adaptability. Each iteration strengthens the network's operational fabric, allowing participants to anticipate, respond to, and learn from failure while preserving dignity, transparency, and continuity. The challenge moving forward lies in calibrating patterns to new scenarios, balancing prescriptive clarity with emergent creativity, and sustaining a field guide that evolves in parallel with the communities it serves.

A path to practice

In October 2020, a small cohort of developers at Aragon in Zug, Switzerland, embarked on a deliberate experiment: each participant assumed a DAO role, interacted with the governance interface, and contributed directly to documentation. Within two weeks, the team had not only completed a functional governance cycle but also identified subtle friction points in voting flows, proposal creation, and permission assignment. By foregrounding direct engagement over abstract discussion, the exercise revealed insights that surveys or speculative design sessions could not. The tangible act of participation transformed theoretical principles into lived understanding, illustrating the potency of small-scale experimentation as a learning modality.

Practical engagement functions as a bridge between comprehension and intuition. Running a wallet, managing a DAO role, or performing a data export anchors abstract concepts in observable behaviour. Participants confront actual latency, UX ambiguities, and error states, gaining immediate feedback on both personal understanding and system design. For example, contributing to Aragon's documentation allowed developers to appreciate how clarity, narrative flow, and reproducibility impact new user experience. By connecting action to consequence, iteration becomes not merely corrective but instructive: each small step generates data points, metrics, and qualitative signals that inform subsequent practice.

The ethos of patient iteration underpins effective learning. Aragon's experiment did not aim for perfection; participants were encouraged to fail gracefully, note deviations, and propose incremental improvements. Metrics such as time-to-complete a proposal, error frequency in wallet interactions, and clarity scores for documentation entries captured both efficiency and comprehension. These indicators, paired with qualitative observation, allowed teams to balance usability, security, and governance fidelity. Limiting the scope to manageable experiments mitigated cognitive overload, maintained engagement, and ensured that each insight could be acted upon without being lost in scale or complexity.

Experimentation in small units exposes friction and opportunity simultaneously. Running a wallet for recurring payments reveals nuances in session management, transaction confirmation, and security prompts. In 2019, ConsenSys' MetaMask team observed that new users consistently hesitated at gas fee configuration, prompting the introduction of gasless onboarding and clearer defaults. Similarly, assigning DAO roles to first-time participants surfaces confusion around permissions and delegation, highlighting design areas where visual cues, progress indicators, or helper text could improve comprehension. These controlled, low-risk exposures function as micro-labs, quantifying both trust and cognitive load in real environments.

Data exports and audit exercises reinforce accountability and transparency. Participants exporting personal or protocol-level data encounter the tension between privacy, traceability, and usability. Filecoin's Lotus testnet in 2021 required users to export storage proofs and account histories, revealing discrepancies in formatting and recoverability. By measuring metrics such as completeness, format compliance, and time to validate, the network calibrated both UX and backend reliability. Such exercises exemplify how small, concrete tasks illuminate systemic assumptions that might otherwise remain hidden, transforming abstract principles—consent, auditability, recoverability—into measurable outputs.

Contributions to documentation illustrate a complementary axis of learning. Documentation acts as both mirror and scaffolding: contributors clarify their own understanding while simultaneously supporting others. Aragon's mentorship ladder paired documentation tasks with issue labelling and review velocity targets, ensuring that updates were accessible, consistent, and actionable. Metrics included time to merge, reviewer feedback frequency, and newcomer comprehension scores. By codifying these patterns, communities convert ephemeral experience into durable guidance, reinforcing a cycle in which practice generates insight, which in turn informs further practice.

Small experiments also cultivate cultural norms. By participating in low-stakes, observable tasks, contributors internalise expectations for communication, review etiquette, and collaborative problem-solving. Ethereum's testnet deployments routinely use hack weeks to orient developers, surface friction points, and normalise failure as a learning signal. This approach contrasts with high-pressure production rollouts, emphasising that skill development, familiarity with toolsets, and trust in communal processes are cultivated through iterative, hands-on engagement rather than abstract instruction.

Patient iteration ensures that learning compounds over time. Each experiment, no matter how modest, generates patterns that can be codified into checklists, heuristics, or field guides. Metrics such as time-to-safe-state, frequency of rollback events, and completeness of consent receipts allow teams to evaluate efficacy across multiple cycles. Contrasting successes and missteps reveals both effective heuristics and persistent friction, enabling continuous calibration of both technical implementation and social protocols.

Balancing scope and ambition is crucial. Too large an experiment risks cognitive overload; too small, and insights may not generalise. Teams can calibrate by combining a simple wallet interaction with a DAO voting simulation and a documentation contribution, producing a compound view of system behaviour. Metrics track task success, time to value, and qualitative comprehension, while observation captures emergent behaviours, misunderstandings, and points of confusion. By iterating across dimensions—technical, social, and procedural—participants accumulate both breadth and depth of experience.

Ultimately, a path to practice reframes learning as a collective craft. It privileges doing over theorising, embeds reflection into action, and generates observable data to guide iteration. Each wallet created, DAO role assumed, or document improved becomes a node in a distributed network of knowledge. By combining metrics, observation, and structured experimentation, communities transform abstract design principles into resilient, user-informed systems. The ongoing challenge is calibrating these small experiments so that they remain instructive, manageable, and generative, ensuring that each contribution enriches both individual understanding and collective competence.

About the Author

Navin Sarkhel builds tools that help people keep control of their data, identity, and work. After years shipping products inside platform ecosystems, he turned to protocols and open source to reduce lock-in and widen participation. He mentors early teams on governance, privacy, and user experience, and contributes documentation as often as code. Born into a family of engineers and teachers, he grew up with stories of community radio and public libraries shaping civic life; that thread runs through his writing on digital commons. He believes the next internet should reward maintainers, respect human dignity, and make exit easy. When not diagramming flows, he hosts small reading groups where designers and developers test ideas against history, from postal networks to packet switching.

www.ingramcontent.com/pod-product-compliance
Lightning Source LLC
Chambersburg PA
CBHW031345230926
51848CB00002B/400